GANGS OF BRITAIN

The gripping true stories behind Britain's organised crime

WENSLEY CLARKSON

JOHN BLAKE

Published by John Blake Publishing,
The Plaza,
535 Kings Road,
Chelsea Harbour,
London SW10 0SZ

www.johnblakebooks.com

www.facebook.com/johnblakebooks
twitter.com/jblakebooks

First published in paperback in 2008
This revised and updated edition published in 2019

ISBN: 978 1 78606 258 1

British Library Cataloguing-in-Publication Data:

A catalogue record for this book is available from the British Library.

Text design and typesetting by seagulls.net

Printed and bound in Great Britain by Clays Ltd, Elcograf S.p.A.

3 5 7 9 10 8 6 4 2

John Blake Publishing is an imprint of Bonnier Books UK
www.bonnierbooks.co.uk

Contents

Preface

Many of the stories you will find in this book were first published ten years ago, with five new chapters written especially for this edition.

While many of these men and women's operations are still alive and well, the last decade has brought even greater turbulence in Britain's crime world. Knife crime is on the up, the rise of social media has made drugs easier to obtain than ever (and to younger and younger people), and the 'old firm' of gangs are continuing to be replaced by the new, leading to more and more chaos on our streets and trouble reaching further and further into our small towns and villages.

However, when there's money on the line, some things will never change: the men and women you'll read about in *Gangs of Britain* all illustrate the dangers, and vast riches, that can come from operating in the shadows of our criminal world as they watch over their shoulders for old foes and new rivals. Their stories are as fascinating – and disturbing – as ever.

Prologue

I first got involved with the shady world of gangsters when I was working on a book about roadrage killer and underworld kingpin Kenny Noye. At the time, I hardly knew Noye's manor; an area that ran from the old docklands of Bermondsey, south east through London, and into deepest Kent. It's a patch known to local law enforcement as the 'Wild West'. 'What goes in there doesn't always come out,' says one veteran thief taker.

So when I tracked down some real-life villains for this book, I wasn't so surprised that they painted an extraordinary picture of a society within a society where criminals and police exist in their own world with their own rules. Hundreds of professional hits are carried out each year in the name of these gangsters. It's chilling to think that such crimes are committed in Britain today, supposedly one of the most law-abiding countries in the world.

Many of the gangsters featured here live and thrive on the same sort of streets and supposedly respectable suburbs in which most 'normal' people live. In

1

Gangs of Britain, I have tried to take the reader on an authentic, nail-biting, roller-coaster ride through the full, face-on brutality of Britain's underworld in the twenty-first century.

All roads in certain big cities lead to this subculture; even the appalling murder of Stephen Lawrence had a link to gangsters because the father of one of the suspects was an associate of Kenny Noye. During my travels I discovered that Noye had made a phone call from inside prison that allegedly enabled those suspects to walk out of a police station just hours after being arrested. The tentacles of master criminals stretch far beyond anything you could imagine.

As one retired detective told me, 'There are outlaws in Britain who are a law unto themselves. If they've got a problem with the police there's always someone they can call to sort things out.'

Today, drug lords rule most of the important manors. Their runners supply coke, puff and E to hundreds of thousands of drug users every week while they retreat to their million-pound detached mansions in the countryside. Ask any copper and he'll tell you it's true. In the Seventies and early Eighties highly professional teams of armed robbers ruled the underworld. But they soon realised that going across the pavement was a far riskier enterprise than putting 50 grand up for a drug deal that often guaranteed a return of 10 times that figure.

Numerous criminals have told me about the hitmen now constantly in demand for their specialised work. 'All the robbers of the Seventies are now dealing drugs big time. We're talkin' about millions of quid changin' hands every week. That means the rotten apples 'ave to be dealt with. There's no shortage of work for a decent shootist,' one retired cannabis smuggler told me.

He introduced me to a hitman we shall call 'Jake', a charming, charismatic man who at no time made me feel in danger. He assured me his only targets were other criminals. He had a wife, two kids, a house in the countryside and all the same problems as the rest of us. I've kept in touch with Jake and he enjoys the kick of being featured in a book, even though only his closest criminal associates would recognise him. He reckons it'll bring him even more respect on the manor.

In many ways I broke the writer's golden rule of getting too close to some of my subjects in *Gangs of Britain*. I had a few threats from the family of one well-known criminal when they thought I was pushing my luck in the name of research. It ended with a sinister phone call telling me that, 'We know where your kids go to school.' But that was it, thank God. Mind you, as another more friendly villain told me months later, 'If they'd really been after your kids they would hardly have bothered to tell you first, would they?'

Not everyone I've written about in *Gangs of Britain* is all bad. They can be funny and even kind and I tried to portray every aspect of their lives rather than just the predictable hardman mode. Many of them are smart survivors doing what they know best.

Sure, if you spend most of your time ducking and diving around the mean streets you start to see the world differently from other people. You learn to survive by your instincts; you don't trust many people; you don't make light conversation because loose lips can sink ships; you spend each day thinking that your world may be shut down by a sharp-eyed policeman or a sneaky grass; you devise ways and means of keeping ahead of the game. Many of these criminals are undoubtedly trapped in their own little world, but then aren't the rest of us as well?

Introduction

MEN ON A MISSION

HOUNSLOW, WEST LONDON, 6.25AM,
26 NOVEMBER 1983

Only CCTV cameras and spotlights mounted on the walls of Unit 7, a steel and brick-built box on a scruffy trading estate near Heathrow Airport, caught the attention of curious onlookers. But when the huge orange-and-white armoured shutter doors rolled open, the building's real purpose was revealed. Chunky dark-blue Brink's-Mat vans, with barred and tinted black windows, came and went from the well-protected loading bay day and night. Unit 7 wasn't Fort Knox or the Bank of England, but it did hold one of Britain's biggest safes, used to store currency, precious metals and other high-risk consignments often *en route* for Heathrow Airport.

Saturday, 26 November 1983, was pitch black and icy cold as a new early morning shift of workers waited outside, kicking their heels as they blew clouds of mist, waiting for 6.30am to arrive. That was when an automatic timer neutralised the high-tech alarm system, allowing the keys to be inserted without

7

triggering flashing lights, bells and alarms linked with the local police station and other security companies.

Four guards pulled up and greeted each other. A fifth one was late and still hadn't arrived when the man who would supervise the day's work drove up. This so-called 'keyman' entered the unit alone, locking the door behind him and leaving the crew outside while he collected another key which shut down the alarm system covering the perimeter walls and windows. The four guards made their way to the rest room to take off their coats. One of them paused briefly to switch on the radio room aerials and the CCTV cameras before joining his mates.

Just then, the doorbell rang. It was the missing guard. He was ten minutes late. The guards heard the keyman go downstairs to let him in. He said he'd overslept, then, mumbling something about having to use the toilet, he disappeared downstairs again.

It was by now 6.40am.

'Get on the floor or you're fuckin' dead.'

A masked man filling the doorway of the rest area spat out the words in a heavy Cockney accent. He aimed his 9mm Browning automatic straight at the guards. Three of them dived for cover.

The armed blagger was white, about 5ft 8in tall and clean shaven, wearing a trilby and a dark car coat or anorak over a black blazer, black trousers and a black tie. He had on a yellow balaclava hitched up to cover all but his eyes.

For a second or two nothing happened, then the gunman jerked his gun arm upwards and, with a silver blazer button glinting in the light, smashed the shooter down on the head of one guard who hadn't gone to the floor quickly enough. Then he beckoned through the open door to someone waiting outside, and at least three more robbers stormed into the room.

'Lie still and be quiet,' ordered the original blagger, as his henchmen started yanking the guards' arms behind their backs and handcuffing them, then locking their legs together at the shins with heavy-duty masking tape. Cloth bags with strings were then pulled down over the guard's heads and fastened around their necks.

One guard saw enough of the main blagger to spot the herring-bone pattern of his tweed hat and the crispness of his starched white shirt. He even noticed a lock of fair hair sticking out from the balaclava as one of the bags was dropped over his head. Keys and watches were snatched from the guards.

Then another voice spat out, 'Get that radio tuned in. If you hear anythin', tell us.' This geezer was the boss. A radio crackled through frequencies until it tuned into a Met Police wavelength. No alarm calls had been made.

Then the 'keyman' felt his shirt pulled up to his chin and a hand tugging violently at his waistband. 'Breathe in deeply or I'll cut you.' Just then a knife sliced through his belted jeans from the buckle to the crutch. A rag was waved under his nose.

'Do you recognise that smell?'

It was unmistakable. The next instant he felt petrol stinging his tackle.

'Do as I fuckin' say, or I'll put a match to the petrol and a bullet through your fuckin' head. I know where you live. You live in a flat in Ruislip High Street above a TV rental shop. We've been watching you for nine months and settin' this up for twelve. Now, let's get on with it. You've got two numbers.'

It was all over in moments and the alarms were neutralised. The team was in. Inside Unit 7's vault the blaggers found a carpet of drab grey containers, no bigger than shoeboxes, bound with metal straps and labelled with handwritten identification codes. There were sixty boxes, containing 2,670 kilos of gold worth £26,369,778. There were also hundreds of thousands of quid in used banknotes locked in three safes. One pouch contained traveller's cheques worth $250,000. In the other was a stash of polished and rough diamonds worth at least 100 grand.

The atmosphere was buzzing as the team moved the gold out to the side of the loading bay and into their waiting vans. Sure, they'd expected riches but nothing like this. The Brink's-Mat robbery, ruthless in its conception and brilliant in its execution, had just landed them the biggest haul in British criminal history, a caper the tabloids soon labelled 'The Crime of the Century'.

Within 48 hours, Lloyds of London announced they'd pay two million quid for information leading to the return of the Brink's-Mat gold, which had already leapt in value by more than twenty pounds an ounce in the hours since the blagging.

The police soon narrowed down their list of suspects to some of the most notorious gangsters in and around London. They had two folders, each containing twelve photographs of the main men. Amongst those mugshots were a number of the faces you will read about in this book. Many of them were never caught, and most of those tens of millions of pounds have been reinvested in everything from cocaine and ecstasy shipments to brothels and a handful of major blaggings.

'Brink's-Mat made the names and fortunes of many of today's most ruthless gangsters,' says one who should know. 'It's the stuff of legends …'

A2, DARTFORD, KENT, MARCH 1976

The Securicor van had been shadowed all over south east London as it picked up takings from more than a dozen shops. Just as the vehicle drove up the busy A2 dual carriageway towards its depot in Powder-mill Lane, Dartford, a gang of blaggers in two stolen motors forced it off the road.

Brandishing sawn-offs, the team ordered the Securicor guards out of the van and helped themselves to more than £100,000 – big money in those days. The windscreen was smashed with a sledgehammer, but when the robbers started spraying bullets around one of the guards was hit and later died. As passing motorists looked on in amazement, the gang escaped by running up an embankment. A number of motorists even photographed them. The police soon rounded up all the usual suspects. This is the hard-nosed blagging that put the Arif family on the map.

Ozer Arif, then 28 and a mini-cab proprietor of Layard Square, Southwark, was later charged with murder along with two other men. Bekir Arif, then

22 and described as a butcher, of Hawkestone Road, Rotherhithe, had his murder charges withdrawn, but he was also nicked for robbery, stealing cars, possessing guns without certificates and disposing of them.

In May 1977, Ozer Arif pleaded not guilty to the murder charges at the Old Bailey. At the end of a four-week trial the jury also found him not guilty of wounding two other guards with intent to cause them grevious bodily harm and possessing shotguns with intent to commit robbery. Meanwhile, brother Bekir got a five-stretch after coughing to robbery.

Afterwards, the Old Bill proudly announced they had broken the back of the Arifs. They boasted to reporters, 'This is the best news we have had for a long time. We reckon we've nipped them in the bud.'

They couldn't have been more wrong.

After Ozer Arif's acquittal, he threw a 'celebration' party and even sent an invitation to the widow of the guard shot dead during the blagging. As they say in the underworld, he felt he should make a gesture.

The Arif family and their army of associates have gone on to make millions thanks to a series of blaggings, highly lucrative drug-trafficking operations and a whole bunch of legitimate businesses set up with stolen cash.

One retired thief taker, who's spent half a lifetime digging into the Arif family background, told me a few years back that the brothers' father was given a new identity by the British Army in Cyprus when he became an informant for the British back in the Fifties. 'He was given a safe house over here and a new identity. That's how the Arif family came to live in south east London. Bloody ironic, isn't it? We helped set up the Arifs as one of the most awesome gangs of villains ever seen in London.'

* * *

The Arifs first emerged as a force to be reckoned with in the Seventies when the family ran a cafe off Deptford Broadway, right in the heart of their adopted homeland of south east London. Oldest brother, Dogan, soon earned himself a reputation as a geezer with a chirpy sense of humour and a fondness for sticking shooters in people's mouths when he wanted to make an important point.

One of the first times Dogan did this was in a pub in Rotherhithe in 1979. Witnesses swear to this day that he pointed his sawn-off right in his victim's face before panning the weapon at this fellow's shoulder and squeezing the trigger. No one in that boozer remembered seeing a thing when the Old Bill later arrived on the scene.

Frightened witnesses always get so confused, and the Arifs had just created a pub full of frightened witnesses. If the Old Bill had tried to get a photofit from the descriptions provided by those punters, they'd have ended up searching for The Elephant Man.

It was a similar tale when Dogan's kid brother Dennis walked into another tavern in South London and fronted up a geezer who owed him some readies. Dennis pushed his Uzi into this bloke's face before playing a sick and twisted game of pizzicato on the poor bastard's belly with a flick knife. Like all major players, the Arifs use fear as their number one weapon. A lot of folk see them strutting round their manor like medieval warlords, building a reputation as bandits who specialise in violent crimes with maximum profits.

During those early days, the Arifs also built up vast reserves of cash from legitimate businesses such as jewellery and menswear stores, a restaurant and a nightclub. Many wondered why the hell they needed the fix of robbery and drugs when everything straight was coming up roses. Their club – The Connoisseur – was a legendary gaff done out in black and shiny chrome on the Old Kent Road. Every face for miles around wanted to be seen on the premises.

Then Dogan and Dennis ran into a heavy bunch of coke dealers inside The Connoisseur. The Arif boys took it upon themselves to 'confiscate' the merchandise. Turned out these fellows had been transporting the drugs for Mafia men who were not happy when they heard what had happened. Dogan and Dennis barricaded themselves inside the club with submachine guns and spent two tense weeks in a stand-off refusing to budge until all parties had reached a satisfactory agreement.

Dogan even used some of the Arif money to support and manage his own football team, Fisher Athletic. Under his guidance, the Docklands club achieved remarkable success a few years back. They were promoted out of the local league into the GM Vauxhall Conference and, as sponsorship money poured in, they got within a whisper of the old Fourth Division.

In 1988, the police tried to come down on the Arifs like the proverbial ton of truncheons. The cops even set up a special squad, reinforced by men from the customs investigation branch, with the express purpose of getting the Arifs. Chop them off at the kneecaps before they take over south east London. Tens of thousands of quid was chucked around in a bid to grease their rivals' palms.

Then Dogan went and got himself nicked riding shotgun on a lorry that was supposed to contain £8 million quid's worth of puff, although Customs officers had already removed the stash and replaced it with chipboard. Dogan swears blind to this day that he was fitted up for that job. He copped a nine year stretch. His mates still say to this day that he was never on the lorry tracked by the cops and Customs officers. He later appealed against his sentence and it was reduced to three years.

In many of the pubs and bodybuilding gyms of south east London, it's said the Arifs have always been clever at stashing away their millions before the long arm of the law can lay its hands on the money. And the Arifs might have kept a cleaner sheet if Dogan and his brothers hadn't made the fatal error of getting directly involved in their own action.

As one retired blagger explained, 'The geezers who stay out of the nick are the ones who never dirty their own hands. They're the fellows who finance the teams who do the actual blaggings or the drug deals. The Arifs should have taken a step back and avoided direct involvement.'

But behind the scenes Dogan and his boys wanted complete and utter respect so they found themselves obliged to get involved in a few tasty gangland battles as a matter of honour. 'They felt they had no choice but to come out fighting,' says one former Arif associate. 'They wanted other faces on the manor to know they don't take no shit off no one.'

In November 1990, the Arifs hit the headlines once again when brothers Dennis and Mehmet plus brother-in-law Anthony Downer tried to pull off the blagging of a Securicor van in Woodhatch, near

Reigate, in Surrey. But the Sweeney got a tip off and armed police lay in wait when the Arif family members and another sidekick struck. They were all nicked on the spot except for blagger Kenny Baker who was shot dead by the police after he and Mehmet decided not to throw down their weapons. The gang was carrying a Brazilian-made revolver, a 12-bore Browning shotgun, a US Army self-loading Colt, an Enfield Mark II revolver and a Browning 1922 pistol. Later that same day, the Old Bill doorstepped a house in Streatham, South London, where they seized a small arsenal of weapons, including three sawn-offs and a sub-machine gun. Mehmet eventually put his hands up to the attempted blagging but Dennis refused to cough and was later found guilty in court.

What really shocked other south east London faces at the time was that Dennis and Mehmet had even bothered to dirty their hands by going across the pavement when they already enjoyed millionaires' lifestyles on their home turf of south east London. 'It's always baffled us. Why the hell didn't they stay away from the action?' says one old Catford face.

NEW KRAYS SMASHED read the massive front page headline in *The Sun* back in December '91 when those two members of the Arif family were finally sent down after trying to rob that security van carrying £1 million. The police proudly screened video footage of the arrest and tried to suggest that the Arifs were now a spent force. But others knew they were far from dead and buried.

Shortly after the brothers were sent down a heavy-weight contest was declared between a brace of south east London firms, many of whom suspected the other had grassed up the Arifs and their gang of blaggers. Round one kicked off in March 1991, when the Arifs' cousin Abby Abdullah walked into William Hill's bookies in Bagshott Street, Walworth, with his bull-terrier on the end of a lead.

Minutes later, a hitman squeezed off two rounds from his 9mm Browning after Abby was fingered by a helpful punter. Abby had even tried to use another customer in the betting shop as a shield but was shot again in the back as he ran from the premises. He then managed to stagger 400 yards to a friend's house on the Kingslake Estate, where he keeled over at the front door. That's when Abby whispered the names of his alleged killers. Soon half the manor heard he'd named a couple of gangsters.

Unemployed mechanic Ginger Horton, 51, told what happened after he found Abby bleeding on his doorstep. 'Abby gasped, "I've been shot. I've been shot … I'm going. I'm going."' Horton went on, 'He tried to sit on a chair. But he fell off on to the floor with blood gushing out of his back. I pulled his shirt up and saw two small bullet holes – one at the top and one at the bottom of his back. These cowards have murdered one of the nicest blokes you could ever wish to meet. He only got out of prison a couple of years ago after being put away as a teenager. He was on life parole. I don't know what he went in for but I can't believe it's got anything to do with this – it happened so long ago.'

Abby was rushed by air ambulance to the Royal London Hospital, Whitechapel, where he was pronounced dead shortly after arrival. When the news of Abby's death was broken by the Arif brothers to their old man, Yusef, who had treated Abby as a son, he went ballistic and the word revenge was on everyone's lips.

In June 1991, a London face was nicked for the Abby shooting by some out-of-town coppers brought in from a special crime unit. They later claimed he told them, 'I didn't mean him to die. I didn't mean it.'

Then one night a well-known face was shot in the Arif's club, The Connoisseur. This fellow, who survived, naturally refused to say who shot him. Three days later in King's College Hospital he spewed up the bullet that grounded him, only to then promptly swallow it again. 'He wanted to stop us doing forensic tests on it,' one plain clothes cop later helpfully explained. 'And you gotta remember these people like to settle things their own way.'

That shooting undoubtedly contributed towards the gunning down of a well-known villain in the middle of 1991. As he was shot, one of the killers screamed, 'This one's for Abby.'

The plugging of this villain was performed by two fellows wearing ski masks. They've never been fingered, but a lot of people reckon one of them was the legendary Jimmy 'Big Jim' Moody, an East End armed robber who escaped from Brixton nick with IRA man Gerard Tuite in 1980. While on the run, Moody legged it across the Irish Sea and made a living as a freelance hitman who iced at least half a dozen geezers, including some well-known Protestant paramilitaries.

In June 1993, Big Jim Moody paid the ultimate price by being gunned down at The Royal pub in Hackney by a lone gunman.

Down at Parkhurst on the Isle of Wight, Dennis and Mehmet Arif were serving 18 and 22 years for that armed blagging.

One screw explained, 'We are not dealing with a bunch of naughty schoolboys. The regime cannot cope.' And another screw who clashed with the Arif brothers moaned, 'It's a situation beyond control because they [the Arifs] run the wing.' Searches of visitors' toilets often unearth stashes of cannabis, crack and cocaine.

Another screw later told me, 'What d'you expect? Drugs help keep inmates more peaceful a lot of the time. No one wants them pacing their cells getting tense and nasty. It's better if they're chilled out in a daze on their bunks, ain't it?'

Dennis and Mehmet, jailed for that £750,000 security van raid at Woodhatch, Surrey, were even rumoured to have mobiles and a couple of shooters in their cells. Some Parkhurst staff were so spooked they asked for outside protection from the brothers. The screws feared attacks on their families after clashing with the Arifs on D-wing.

One screw explained, 'A prisoner in D-wing head-butted a senior warder so hard his retina was detached. The inmate was segregated but was back in 24 hours because of the Arifs. We were all disgusted.'

Another time, a warden was injured after skidding on two packets of cocaine lying in a corridor (I kid thee not). He was last heard of threatening to sue the prison authority. And those screws who still patrolled the Arifs' wing found they could no longer use the specially installed security viewers to take a look inside cells.

'All the spyholes are blocked by curtains, paint or paper,' groaned one fed-up officer. Dennis and Mehmet are due back out in the real world some time next year.

* * *

In October 1997, two more of the Arif boys, Bekir and Michael, were pulled by detectives investigating a plot to flood the streets with more than £10 million worth of heroin. The police claimed they found 95 kilos of the drug piled up in the front room of a South London house raided by them.

The Old Bill's swoop marked the end of a lengthy undercover operation by Scotland Yard's elite Organised Crime Group which was set up to combat Mafia-style villains like the Arifs. Detectives reckoned Bekir and Michael were running a major drug-trafficking and distribution network. Car dealer Bekir, 44, was charged with conspiracy to supply heroin while Michael Arif was released pending further enquiries.

In May 1999, Bekir, at the time 46-years-old and living in a £250,000 house in Petts Wood, Kent, was jailed for 23 years after being convicted of conspiracy to supply heroin. The court was told that Bekir had used his second-hand car business as a front to supply £12 million worth of heroin.

The court also heard that the cops had spent a year watching his car business in Rotherhithe and a nearby flat. The jury were even played tapes of conversations recorded by sophisticated listening devices and shown photos of the main players in action.

In court Bekir, known by now as 'The Duke', insisted he was nothing more than a 'Del Boy' businessman. It didn't help when prosecutors pointed out Bekir was splashing out 30 grand a year for an executive box to watch the Arsenal. Judge Geoffrey Grigson told Bekir, 'Your role was plainly that of principal and your conduct was as cynical and dishonest as has been your defence. In my view there is no mitigation.'

* * *

I met up with Dogan Arif at his business address, a fruit and ciggie machine service centre in a dead-end street, just off the Old Kent Road. 'I'll see you on the cameras and come and get you,' he told me on the phone an hour before our meet. As I drove my old jalopy slowly towards a brick wall that marked the end of the road, I wondered what he really meant. The idea of Dogan Arif coming to get me sent a shiver up my spine.

In the not too distant past, Dogan's favourite way of getting anyone's attention had been to stick a shooter in their face and ask questions later. As one-time unofficial godfather of the Arif family, his reputation precedes him with everyone from the major faces in London to the police at Scotland Yard. Dogan is respected by them all – a true guv'nor of guv'nors.

The CCTV cameras that pan the end of the lane where he has his one-armed bandit warehouse command a view of rundown buildings and lots of broken glass shattered across the pavement. It's just a stone's throw from their old club, The Connoisseur. As I slung my old Merc up on the kerb, a Doberman the size of a small donkey came bounding out of a side-door.

Just then a tall, dark-haired, bull-necked bouncer-type yanked the pooch back into the front office of the warehouse. Inside, a pretty girl in her early twenties offered me a cuppa and told me that Dogan would be out 'any minute'. It was all very civilised.

Then the man himself emerged grinning and full of charm. He walked me through the small warehouse, filled with flashing machines, into his office. Compact, muscular and moving with an athlete's roll, I was instantly reminded that he was once a talented footballer. Many reckon Dogan could have made it as a pro, but he had bigger fish to fry.

It turned out Dogan was still miffed about how he'd been nicked for that £8 million puff deal back in 1988. His brief reckoned if he'd been anyone else the conviction would have been completely thrown out. Dogan shrugs his shoulders when he tells you this. That's the way it goes, ain't it?

Back then, Dogan claimed, the police confiscated everything, including half the family mansion in Catford. They even closed down his pride and joy – The Connoisseur. As Dogan later told me, 'I didn't have a penny when I got out in July 1993. For six months I did nothing. I was lost. Three years is a lot of time to sort your head out, set out your stall in life.'

Dogan told me he'd turned over a new leaf. Gone straight. But it's not easy teaching an old dog new tricks. Behind the charming smile, Dogan's old brain was churning over more money-making schemes than Al Pacino in *Scarface*. One old thief taker I know still calls him to this day, 'the thinking man's gangster'. While Dogan was banged up in Parkhurst the governor even encouraged him to talk to prison visitors because he had such a sharp take on life inside. He's a smart fellow, knows how to spin a neat sentence together and he's got a superb take on life.

'Sometimes it'd be nice to wipe out the past,' Dogan told me. 'But you can't do that, can you? People never let you forget. That's just the way it is. You have to take life on the chin.'

When I met Dogan he said everything he was into was purely legit; leasing cigarette vending machines and assorted one-armed bandits to pubs and clubs throughout south east London. But it's difficult to imagine that his reputation doesn't impress the customers. 'I split the profits of each machine fifty/fifty with the owner of every place I supply.'

Of course, the Old Bill on the manor insisted Dogan was only keeping a low profile because he knew he'd cop a 15-year stretch next time around. 'I couldn't handle that,' Dogan admitted to me. Only a few weeks before our meet, Dogan had popped down to Parkhurst to see his old mate Eddie Richardson while he was visiting brothers Mehmet and Dennis.

Dogan said that drugs were rotting the very core of gangsterdom. He reckoned about 80% of those faces heavily involved in drug deals are taking the same poison they're peddling. 'That makes a lot of them unstable. All the rules have been thrown out the window. You can't predict anythin'. These chaps are out of control. It's like an army no one can command. How can you control people who can't control themselves? There's no respect, no code any more. Years ago I might pick up the phone and say, "Look, that mustn't happen. Cut it out." Now, the chances are they'll say, "Who the hell are you? Piss off!" The game's changed. The chaps are no longer in control.'

Dogan reckoned the big families of the Eighties and Nineties were on the way out. 'They had principles and respect. The police could keep things under control 'cause people were predictable. Now there are hundreds of operators all over the place climbin' on the bandwagon. It's too easy by half. Let's say Billy Bloggs has a transport company. He'll move a consignment of drugs. Suddenly he's got more money than he's ever dreamed of. Now he's in the underworld. He's got to have soldiers. But he doesn't know what he's doing, he knows nothin' about it, but he's in it. It's chaos. There's no respect and no control. You can't blame the public if they want the police to throw the rules out of the window. And they do. They infiltrate, they pay big money to grasses. There's electronic surveillance, MI5. If you have things you care about – a family – don't even think about it any more.'

Dogan sounded convincing. At the time I met him he was definitely trying to stay on the straight and narrow and avoid the limelight. But that didn't stop him being asked for his opinions in certain south east London taverns where he remains a respected hardman, a feared gangster who knows what's what.

'I get pestered by people who want to talk about the old days the minute I walk into certain places. It drives me mad. They call up the champagne, slap me on the back. I'd rather have a bottle of wine at home with my family.'

Dogan blamed a lot of it fairly and squarely at the feet of the OTT 1980s. 'Everyone had money in the Eighties. Everyone was spending like crazy. There'd be kids with five grand in their pocket. They'd say, "Give us a gram of Charlie. What the hell, make it five grams." They'd ask me for it. I'd sling them out, the idiots.'

Despite his family being linked to the supply of mountains of drugs, Dogan swore blind he was fiercely anti-narcotics. 'When I was a kid I was in the jungle. There is only one way out of the jungle – you fight your way out. But I've done it. That stuff is a killer, believe me.'

Dogan reckoned his legit businesses, his family and Fisher Athletic FC were all that mattered to him now. The club slipped back into obscurity during his stretch in the nick. But by the time I caught up with him, Dogan had returned as technical director and he was convinced he could help lead Fisher back to the glory days.

Then our conversation turned to one of the Nineties' most notorious south east London gangsters, whose name was top of all the Most Wanted Lists. 'He's bad news for all of us. He caused us a lot of heat and I hope he's six feet under 'cause we can do without his kind,' Dogan said. 'Where I come from you keep things low key. You don't draw attention to yourself in the way this fellow has. Sure, I've met him in the past but he's not someone I'd ever do business with.'

Dogan says that the gangster is motivated by greed and drugs. 'Fuckin' drugs have caused a lot of these problems. Now the stakes are so fuckin' high that knockin' off a chap is done without anyone even givin' a toss. It's tragic and we're all goin' to end up six feet under at this rate. We're all destroying ourselves.'

Meanwhile some of Dogan's brothers may be currently under lock and key but rest assured their fortune hasn't disappeared. As one recently retired cop told me recently, 'We'll be lucky if we get our hands on a tenth of their money. They've been clever at distributing it. And once they're out they'll no doubt be involved in all sorts of nonsense.'

Despite a few local difficulties, the Arif brothers – Ozer, Dennis, Mehmet and Dogan – are far from dead and buried having copped a multi-million-pound fortune thanks to the lucrative drugs trade that mushroomed in the late Eighties and early Nineties.

'Sure, there are other tasty characters on the manor these days, but these guys have still got a fearsome reputation,' says one old lag.

The Arifs are not to be crossed ...

Chapter 2

COCKY

Curtis 'Cocky' Warren, complete with Desperate Dan pecs and a head shaved as round and smooth as a billiard ball, virtually has the word 'Gangster' stamped across his forehead. In some ways he's so obvious no one can take his reputation seriously. But many villains have found out to their cost that Cocky Warren is a deadly character with blood as cold as ice.

Cocky's one smart cookie. Streetwise, low key and very bright – and he's only in it for the very big money. This is a character who has dealt in hundreds of thousands of pounds worth of drugs every week.

As his arch enemies, the police, now openly admit, 'He might be nothin' much to look at, the usual Scouse lad in a shell suit, but he's one helluv an operator. He doesn't drink, smoke or use drugs. He's got a photographic memory for telephone numbers, bank accounts and the like. We've been looking for where he keeps his stuff. On a computer? In notes? No way. He carries it all inside his head.'

His nickname comes from 'Cocky Watchman' which is Scouse slang for a dodgy character. And in Liverpool he's been known for years as the Colombian Cali cartel's *primera* agent in northern Europe. This gangster is pure and utter evil and he's one of the richest villains in the land. He even made it on to *The Sunday Times* Rich 500 list, the highest placed gangster ever to do so.

Cocky Warren makes the Krays look like amateurs. The Great Train Robbery and Brink's-Mat geezers, swaggering highwaymen from the pre-drugs era, are nothing more than second division. Curtis Warren is Premier League.

The key to Cocky's success is that until he came on the scene most villains got their drug shipments via middlemen. That meant they dealt in relatively small quantities. One hundred kilos was a major seizure for Customs and Excise ten years ago. Then Curtis Warren came on the scene and those smalltime operators soon faded into the background.

Cocky rapidly got himself a direct line to the biggest drug cartels in all four corners of the universe. Charlie from the Colombians; puff from the growers and fields of Morocco and Senegal; Europe's finest quality amphetamines and E from the top labs, mainly in Holland; and heroin from the poppy fields of Afghanistan.

And once Cocky had got the right financial backing he didn't even have to bother with cash upfront. Suppliers gave him virtually unlimited credit once he proved he could lay his hands on the cash. He'd get a shipment and then sell on a third of it to drug dealers in other European countries so that he was already in profit before his team hit the streets of Liverpool with the produce.

In his early days, the late Eighties, Cocky had been known for waving shooters in people's faces, but by the time the Nineties came around he was so powerful that he left all that to his team. No one crossed Cocky.

Smuggling coke, puff, smack and E was Cocky's full-time profession and he'd studied the best methods as closely as a scientist preparing a vaccine for cancer.

In Britain last year around £500 million worth of narcotics was seized by customs and police, but that's not even 5% of the gross national product. It's a trade worth tens of billions of pounds. Cocky Warren is the kingpin; a bulk buyer who knows exactly how to deal with the heaviest. 'Cocky's a man of honour. He never backs out once he's cut a deal and the Colombians reckon he is *numero uno*,' said one who should know.

The drug barons thrive because of one simple premise: supply and demand. More people snort a line, pop a pill or take a puff on a joint than ever before. A lot of them might call it stress relief, but all they're doing is lining the pockets of some of the most deadly faces this country has ever known.

The police keep trying to chip away at the gangsters but it's not easy. Cocky Warren and his crew have shelled out hundreds of thousands of quid in bribes to bent cops. And whenever the straight cops get close they seem to just fail at the final hurdle.

Cocky and his team reckon no amount of policing will ever wipe them out – and the vast profits continue to roll in. Even when multi-millionaire gangsters like Cocky are taken off the street and locked up their power and influence continues and their stashes of cash get bigger and bigger. Cocky has a long chain of command and no one dares cross him.

Cocky Warren's first brush with the law as a major dealer came in the late Eighties when one of his couriers was stopped at Dover with a Bible which had been hollowed out and packed with heroin. Persuaded to help the Old Bill, Warren's soldier went and called his boss at home and told him he 'had the drugs'. The phone line went dead before Cocky could incriminate himself. There was no case against him, but he was now a target for the cozzers. Cocky Warren, without a qualification to his name and apparently without a job, was heading for the sort of riches most of us can only dream about.

It was all a very different story when Curtis Francis Warren was born at home in Liverpool on 31 May

1963. His old man was a mixed-race sailor with the Norwegian Merchant Navy. His grandfather is even listed as a coffee manufacturer in the Americas. His mum, Sylvia Chantre, is the daughter of a shipyard boiler attendant.

Cocky was brought up in the Granby district of Toxteth, a bomb-damaged area of Liverpool wiped out by the Jerries during the last war and then re-flat-tened by the Toxteth riots in the early Eighties. When he was 12 he was nicked for joyriding. It's a hard manor where only the tough survive. Cocky quit school in his early teens and soon found himself in more trouble with the law for petty thieving. Then he honed his criminal skills snatching handbags and dealing in small amounts of puff.

He even hung around outside the gates of his old school selling wraps of heroin to local junkies. And he was picking up friends and acquaintainces as fast as a kerb crawler. One mate, Mike Ahearne, ended up on the TV show *Gladiators*. Another pal was Johnny 'Sonny' Phillips, a black bouncer who went on to became a fearsome enforcer – one of the tough-est characters in Liverpool. Another mate was Stephen Mee, who later made a daring escape from a prison van in the middle of the Yorkshire moors.

The cops in Liverpool say Cocky soon moved up the criminal ladder by working on club doors as a bouncer. Then he began running a team of heavies organising security for various taverns. As one of his old mates explained, 'If you control the doors, you control the drugs.'

In 1988 came Cocky's biggest break. He hooked up with a notorious Liverpool businessman, known as 'The Banker' who'd made his first fortune hijacking lorries at Liverpool docks back in the Sixties. Half of Merseyside reckons The Banker had been backing drug operations on the manor for years. Renowned for his involvement in loads of crimes but without a nicking to this day. The Banker helped Warren make the leap from local supplier to regional trafficker by giving him the financial clout to steam in to the big drug boys. Cocky had serious ambitions to be the main wholesaler for the whole of north west England. Those who dealt with Cocky at the time knew he was a good operator. 'He's ultra-intelligent, as sharp as they come,' says his one-time brief, Kevin Dooley.

Within months, Cocky Warren became totally immersed in the coke trade, bigtime. Then he teamed up with another drug baron who worked the north east of England to Cocky's north west. These two characters pulled in so much dosh that they became multi-millionaires virtually overnight.

Jealous small-time gangsters across Liverpool started grassing up Cocky Warren's activities so he decided to nurture some important boys in blue. Merseyside senior detective Chief Inspector Elmore Davies, later jailed for five years for corruption for his part in trying to get one of Cocky's acquaintances off a firearms charge, was just one of Cocky's new best friends.

Then in September 1991, Cocky stepped on to the global drug stage when he and the drug baron travelled from Dover to Calais by ferry on British visitor passports. Accompanying them was Mario Halley, a 'marketing representative' for the Cali cartel in Colombia. Cocky and his two mates told immigration they were only travelling inside Europe. Then they drove to Brussels, where they parked their car before catching a plane to Malaga, Spain. From Malaga they went up to Madrid. Then Cocky and his accomplice took out their own ten-year regular passports and flew across to Caracas, Venzuela, which just happens to share its border with Colombia.

In South America, Warren was introduced to Camillo Jesus Ortiz, who headed up a company formed on behalf of the cartel – the Conar Corporation. Warren and his mate put down a £6 million deposit for two giant shipments of Charlie. The first, of 1.5 tonnes, would arrive in the port of Felixstowe the following month, October 1991. The coke would be hidden in steel boxes sealed inside lead ingots, which were not easy to slice open and impossible to X-ray.

Just before the shipment arrived, Cocky Warren flew to Amsterdam with two of his associates Anthony Cahill, 26, and Colin Smith to discuss the final details of the shipment. The team were re-introduced to Colombian Jesus Ortiz by the cartel's marketing man Mario Halley. Within days Warren and his team were given the nod that their goods were on the way and Mario Halley flew into Manchester where he was driven to Merseyside by Cocky to await the shipment.

Cocky and Halley arrived with special tools to remove 500kg of Charlie which Warren would then distribute in Britain, while the rest went to Holland and Greece. Cocky's distribution deal guaranteed he was already in profit before he'd even flogged a gram of his coke on Merseyside.

But before the shipment left Felixstowe, Dutch cops tipped off British customs that a major shipment of drugs was hidden in steel boxes inside the lead ingots. Customs even cut open one ingot in that first shipment from South America but found nothing.

The ingots were released and taken to a warehouse outside Liverpool. South American Halley was on site to extract the cocaine. The ingots were then buried in rubble at a mill before being sold for scrap, ending up in Newcastle.

A second shipment, of 900kg, left Venezuela in December that year. As it came in Cocky Warren and his accomplice were nicked. It looked as if the law had them bang to rights this time. But then certain cops, whose identities were never known, came forward and claimed the accomplice was an informer and should be given special treatment. They insisted he should be allowed to walk free so he could put the finger on some even bigger fish. The boys in blue eventually torpedoed the Customs' entire case. The accomplice was released and the case against Cocky Warren and Anthony Cahill at Newcastle Crown Court collapsed in 1992.

Cocky was so chipper he spat at the Customs officers who'd pursued him: 'I'm off to spend my £87 million from the first shipment and you can't fuckin' touch me.' He boasted to associates that a number of his police contacts got handsomely rewarded for their unswerving loyalty after the case against him was thrown out.

Cocky's acquittal in Newcastle also sent a message to the cartels he dealt with across the globe. They now knew that, although Cocky had faced decades in the slammer, he'd kept his mouth shut. He'd never once offered to do a deal and turn grass. This was a man to be trusted. Being nicked was the best thing that ever happened to Cocky.

Certain straight-shooting cops, however, remained determined to nick him. Less than six months later, Customs officers conducted a covert search of a lorry at Felixstowe and found 250kg of heroin. They watched as it was driven to Burton Wood services on the M62; then, while it was parked, they saw Cocky drive into the compound. But then he spotted the surveillance officers and scarpered. 'He's got this built-in radar system – it's called his brain. He reckons he can sense any problems before they happen,' says one old associate.

Customs were naturally hopping mad. Both sides made important decisions that day. Customs launched Operation Crayfish to try and land the biggest fish of all – Curtis Warren. He was to get 24-hour round-the-clock surveillance with all the trimmings. And Cocky knew he'd need to have that radar switched on 24-hours-a-day.

Not long afterwards, £30,000 of Cocky's money was confiscated by the Old Bill during a raid on an associate's property. The small-time gangsters soon found the cash elsewhere and paid up Cocky within days. That's what villains call respect.

When the Moroccan Government tried to put the squeeze on the puff industry, Cocky flew over to North Africa and went out and bought people off; hotel staff, bankers and a bunch of coppers. 'That's what we call real class. He knew the key to his survival was greasing the right palms. It's what makes him such a big-time player,' says one in the know.

Cocky even tried to keep his motors low key. He was usually only seen out and about in a black Nexus, aircon as standard. He told one associate, 'It doesn't do you any good to be seen flashing it around. It winds people up.'

In the spring of 1995, Cocky's main man, Johnny Phillips, walked into a rundown Liverpool bar called Cheers and had a face-off with rival gangster, David Ungi, a former amateur boxing champ. Phillips, a steroid-pumping giant, was well pissed off at Ungi and told Cocky that Ungi deserved a good hiding 'or worse'.

On 1 May 1995, Ungi was shot dead at the wheel of his motor. It later emerged that a previous attempt to kill him had failed. A spate of shoot-outs followed the Ungi killing. Phillips himself was hit and seriously wounded in one attack. Although he survived, Phillips died the following year from heart failure after years of steroid and Charlie abuse.

Following the Ungi shooting, Liverpool descended into all-out gang war. That month – May 1995 – 11 people were shot. Yet virtually nobody was nicked. One fellow was sliced up so badly with a machete that it took seven hours for the coroner to join his body parts together in order to carry out a half-decent autopsy.

The Wild-West-style antics of the drug-fuelled gangsters on the streets of his home town really got up Cocky Warren's nose. He quit Merseyside and set up home in Holland, although the police believe to this day that he was behind a lot of the shoot-outs himself. 'I think he realised that if he hung around someone was going to have a pop at him. Things were getting way too hot for him,' one detective says today.

Typically, Cocky Warren was soon running his drugs empire from Holland. Early in 1996 Customs intercepted 60 kilos of coke hidden inside a petrol tanker at Dover which they're convinced was *en route* to Cocky. Police also linked Cocky to a half ton of puff seized at another British port around the same time.

Cocky then decided to devise a more airtight system. He knew he had to stop taking any personal risks otherwise he'd end up under permanent lock and key. So shortly after arriving in Holland, Cocky set up a cellular network of drugs with each section working independently of the other. That meant if one part of the Warren organisation was busted then it wouldn't affect any of the other sections.

Cocky had settled in a modest Dutch town called Sassenheim in a villa called Bakara. He hung a boxer's punchbag from the attic ceiling and checked out the world from four slits in the roof. North, east, south and west were always covered. All alone in the big house with virtually no furniture, Warren spent hours every day gossiping to his old team back in Merseyside. What he didn't realise was that every call was being monitored by the Dutch police although he was smart enough never to refer to anyone by their real name – nicknames only.

They sounded like something out of an Elmore Leonard crime novel; The Vampire, Cracker, Macker and Tacker the Bell with no Stalk, the Egg on Legs, Lunty, Badger, Boo, Twit and Twat, Big Foot, the Big Fella, the J Fella, the L Fella and many more.

One time Warren gently stepped in between two brothers at the centre of a feud back in Liverpool. He talked to his family. It was clear Cocky missed Merseyside and, typically, despite already being a very rich man, he couldn't resist wheeling and dealing. He thrived on the excitement. In some ways, the buzz gave him more of a kick than the readies.

So while Curtis Warren was busy re-organising his empire, Operation Crayfish – 30 cops working full time to bring Cocky to justice – continued shadowing his every move. They wanted to pick off each of Cocky's commercial limbs, one by one. With the help of underworked spies at MI5 they stepped up surveillance to include phone taps and round-the-clock electronic intelligence gathering.

They believed one of the keys to nicking Cocky was to break up his swift and superbly organised money-laundering system, in which he cleverly manipulated currency exchange rates to cleanse tens of millions of pounds each year.

Meanwhile, Cocky Warren lived up to his reputation as a non-smoking teetotaller, who has probably still never tried any of the narcotics he's sold for such a vast profit. Despite being in Holland, he remained close to his girlfriend, Stephanie Glennon, the mother of his child. He even owned a private jet, as well as learning to fly helicopters, and indulged himself in loads of chunky gold jewellery.

And Cocky Warren showed immense generosity to those who did what he wanted. From Holland he paid out £50,000 each to two witnesses in a shooting trial of a close associate. Cocky even arranged for a Liverpool bodyguard to give £10,000 to his favourite detective via his old school pal and one-time *Gladiators* TV star Mike Ahearne.

Dutch police monitoring Cocky's phones tipped off Merseyside police and they dropped a camera into Warren's friend's flat, gathering enough evidence to bring about a successful prosecution of that bent copper. Ahearne was eventually jailed for being the go-between for Cocky and the corrupt cop.

A few months after setting up shop in Holland, Cocky sent one of his dodgier pals, Stephen Mee, already on the run from a 22-year sentence following an earlier escape from a prison van on the Pennines, to

Colombia to arrange a 400kg shipment of Charlie. It was to be packed inside metal ingots just like the ones all those years earlier. Cocky reckoned the law would never think he'd try and use the same method of shipment. What he didn't realise was that a little birdie had already told the Old Bill that Cocky was about to pull off this Charlie deal.

Cocky dreamt up a scheme to import the drugs to Bulgaria through his 'wine interests'. The coke would be cooked into liquid and – here's the clever bit – then held in suspension inside bottles of Bulgarian red plonk. Then it would be shipped back across Europe to Warren's beloved Merseyside where it would be banged out at a 2,000 per cent mark-up.

First the Charlie turned up at Cocky's Dutch hacienda in a container filled with those lead ingots. That's when Holland's version of the SAS moved in with stun grenades and busted Cocky and his team. Moments after the Dutch SWAT team smashed down his front door, they found Cocky in bed with a busty Ukranian hooker.

Many hours of drilling holes in metal ingots followed before more than 400 kilos of pure Colombian marching powder was uncovered. At six other addresses lived in by Warren's mates, Dutch police found millions of pounds' worth of other drugs and enough weaponry to start a civil war. By the time they'd counted it all up, the Dutch cops reckoned they'd bagged £125 million worth of drugs.

Cocky Warren's trial in Holland was even switched at short notice to a secret location after Dutch police got wind of a plan to spring Cocky from jail. The change in venue was so sudden it left dozens of British reporters watching proceedings on a screen in the Paleis Van Justitie. At first the Dutch authorities refused to say where the trial was to be conducted. Cocky had provoked a lot of fear and trepidation.

When the trial finally got under way, Cocky denied six charges relating to specific quantities of drugs and to the illegal possession of firearms. The most serious charge was that Cocky had masterminded the trafficking operation from his mansion in Sassenheim. His two old mates from the UK, Stephen Mee and Stephen Whitehead, stood with him in the dock.

At one stage proceedings were halted after claims that evidence against Cocky 'may have been contaminated'. His brief, Han Jahae, claimed that British investigators had illegally tapped into Cocky's phones rendering the Dutch prosecution null and void. Jahae also insisted that evidence used against Cocky in that early Newcastle trial, in which he had been acquitted, should not be used in this latest case.

Cocky was even allowed to issue a statement after the Dutch judge adjourned the case while four extra witnesses were located. He told reporters, 'It's important that you investigate how the English got their information. Why did they need to claim public immunity?'

Cocky finally copped a 12-year stretch in Holland and the judge made a point of telling the court that he had not given him the maximum 16-year sentence because Warren did not belong to 'the extremely violent drugs barons'. Many would no doubt disagree with that statement. Cocky wasn't in court for his sentencing but he'd already dismissed the charges against him as being 'a police set-up'.

Britain's Customs and Excise put on a brave face. 'An entire drugs gang has been destroyed,' said Paul Acda, deputy chief. 'Warren was a unique trafficker in British terms, because he had direct contact with the sources of the drugs. It will take a long time before anybody takes his place.'

Cocky knew he would have received double the sentence back in Britain, although the police in Britain concede it would have been a nightmare trying to find a jury who wouldn't have ended up being intimidated by Cocky's pals. And don't forget that some of his closest mates also happened to be members of the constabulary.

Even from his prison cell, however, Cocky Warren continued to have his finger in a lot of pies. He'd boasted of owning Barrow Football Club's ground. The police believed he also invested heavily in a number of football league clubs. And the Football Association have even helped the Customs and police with their enquiries into Cocky's activities.

The National Crime Squad spent many months probing Cocky's links with Stephen Vaughan, Barrow FC's former chairman and owner who resigned in late 1998. While there's no suggestion that Vaughan was connected to any of Cocky's criminal activities, there was concern about Cocky using some of his millions to keep the club afloat.

Vaughan bought the club in 1995 and was widely credited with saving it from going down the pan. But 18 months later he was questioned about his links to Cocky Warren and claims that the club had been fraudulently purchased. Vaughan admits knowing Cocky, but insists that's only because he had at one time employed Warren's security company for his boxing promotions.

Vaughan also admitted, 'He [Warren] once put £17,500 into my solicitor's account to buy a council house I wanted to sell, but the deal never went through and I gave him his money back. I did buy a Toyota Land Cruiser from him.'

There were rumours in Merseyside that Cocky Warren and a consortium of associates were trying to buy a controlling stake in one of the first division's top sides. But after the club heard about the Curtis Warren connections they refused to meet the group of 'businessmen'. Cocky was so narked by the club's attitude that he was now even more determined to target a top club. One of his former associates explained, 'Cocky sees soccer as the ultimate ego trip. He wants to control a club because he likes the idea of the powerbase and it is also a great way to launder a lot of dirty money.'

During the police investigation into Cocky's links to certain football clubs, they launched a separate inquiry into his father-in-law Philly Glennon, nicknamed the Silver Fox. They believed that he'd also made a fortune out of drug dealing. When Merseyside detectives paid a visit to Glennon's home they found more than £1 million in cash buried in his back garden. Glennon was described at the trial of Cocky's favourite bent cop as a 'wealthy crook who made his money through drugs'.

The police even discovered that an off-shore company gave one football club connected to Cocky a £300,000 loan even though the company did not appear to have ever traded. Police also unearthed evidence that cash from drugs deals had been laundered through a bunch of property transactions involving an investment company based in the Isle of Man.

Cocky first came up with the idea of taking over a football club after visiting his Cali cartel cronies in Colombia, where drug barons moved into the soccer business years ago. In one notorious incident the cartel shot national team defender Andrés Escobar after he scored an own goal in the World Cup in 1994.

Meanwhile, Cocky was banged up in the maximum security prison at Vught, on the site of a former Nazi concentration camp in Holland. During the first few months after he was sent down, other inmates said he was a quiet prisoner steering clear of trouble. He knew that outside those four walls dozens of cops were working round the clock to track down his tens of millions of pounds. When Customs officials got wind of rumours that at least £10 million of Cocky's money had been secretly deposited in a Swiss bank account he shrugged his shoulders and told one associate, 'It's a small price to pay.'

But Cocky's influence continued to reach far beyond the bars of his Dutch prison cell. Greater Manchester police nicked one of their own officers shortly after Cocky's incarceration and accused him of helping the megawealthy gangster to launder millions of pounds in drugs cash.

Back in Merseyside the run-down streets remained paved in gold thanks to Cocky and his team of dealers and suppliers. Amid many boarded-up shops, deserted streets and the faded grandeur of a bygone era there were bizarre pockets of immense wealth in Liverpool; flashy nightclubs; designer clothes shops. Official statistics suggested a city on the edge of financial ruin. But out on the streets, Cocky was considered a Robin Hood-style hero who provided vast salaries for hundreds of people feeding off the massive profits of drug dealing.

Flashy limos cruised the streets and virtually every kid on a street corner seemed to own a mobile, not a common sight back then. Even the much respected *North-West Business Insider*, a regional business magazine, declared drugs were behind most of the city's small business success stories. It was reckoned Warren's team were still shifting 500kg of drugs each and every month.

Just have a think about this statistic: a police raid on a ship in Rotterdam at that time uncovered 800kg worth of Charlie with a street value of £75 million. In other words, that 500kg was worth at least £46 million a month – big money in anyone's terms.

And Cocky's empire had long since spread to London, the Midlands and Scotland. As Steve Brauner, editor of *North-West Business Insider*, said, 'He's like a broker in legal commodities. He negotiates a price with the suppliers – in this case the Colombian cocaine cartel – before selling on several slices of the consignment at a mark-up to other criminal organisations.

The profit on those deals mean he's getting the rest of the consignment for nothing. His profit on any drugs brought into this country is 100 per cent.'

In the summer of 2000, Cocky's team ordered a steady stream of travellers clutching sports bags to board buses and trains from Liverpool to London. Mingling with tourists, they then exchanged cash sums as high as £500,000 at Bureaux de Change in the capital. Much of it was changed into large denomination notes of Dutch gilders or German marks. That money was then carefully banked in offshore tax havens. The couriers from Liverpool are bunged £300 a time for their journey south. They'd never dare to do a runner with the loot. 'It's more than their life's worth,' says one who knows.

Cocky's biggest problem has always been to get the money back from his offshore accounts to Merseyside. In later years he cracked that problem by backing small businesses with loans. The father of one of Warren's police mates even helped him set up a string of small companies which appeared to lack any income yet held money in the bank. Cocky naturally kept his name out of all documentation. There's no Inland Revenue record, nor has he ever claimed any benefit. Even the fancy mansion he owns out in posh Hoylake, north of Liverpool, was bought in the name of a dead man with no dependents.

His numerous terraced houses in Liverpool appeared to belong to a respectable property company – except that it was in receipt of a mysterious offshore loan for £2 million and no one would say who lent them the money. Cocky's never been too keen on paperwork. Before he was banged up in Holland he'd turn up at companies he wanted to 'invest' in with a bag of readies usually stuffed with at least £500,000. There were never any papers to sign so nothing could link Cocky to his business loans scheme.

So, while Cocky continues serving his time, back in Liverpool the gangs who virtually blasted each other to oblivion in the mid-1990s don't even dare to try and reclaim Cocky's turf. He's been above such local difficulties for years and no one will cross him. Yet ironically, Cocky had been trying to broker a peace deal between warring Jamaicans and other street dealers when he got sent down by the court in Holland.

The Merseyside police effort to carve up Cocky's territory and break the other drug cartels in Liverpool looks doomed to failure. Customs officers have even been forced to base their own investigation at least 30 miles outside the city for their own safety. Customs planning raids have been told by local cops they cannot guarantee their safety. Despite being heavily armed and carefully targeting specific gangsters they know that any unknown motor near a villain's house on Merseyside will be spotted by kids with mobile phones, often supplied by Cocky's team.

In June 1999, Cocky launched an appeal against his Dutch prison sentence. His lawyers insisted British security officers illegally passed on info to the Dutch police. They even claimed they could win a retrial in front of a new judge and threatened to take the case to the European Court of Human Rights.

Then in September 1999, Cocky found it wasn't so easy being banged up after all. He got himself into some heavy-duty aggro which ended up with him flooring a mad Turk who came at him with a knife and a head butt. The poor bastard ended up dead after Cocky lashed out with a couple of killer punches.

Guards at the prison insisted Cocky was first headbutted by his fellow inmate, 37-year-old Turkish cellmate Gema Guclu. Curtis then punched him back and within seconds they were hitting out and kicking each other and rolling over on the ground. Screws quickly cleared other prisoners out of their cells and into a secure unit, ignoring Cocky's deadly bare-knuckle dust-up. They later said it would have been too dangerous to separate the men fighting while other prisoners were 'in the immediate vicinity'.

A Dutch Justice Ministry spokewoman said, 'When the guards returned they saw Curtis Warren standing over the other man, who was lying on the ground, obviously badly injured.' The Turk was rushed to hospital and put on a life support machine, but he died the following day from a brain haemorrhage.

For months officials wouldn't confirm whether the con died as a result of being hit by Cocky or whether his haemorrhage was caused by the Turk head-butting Cocky! Cocky's Manchester-based brief Keith Dyson said at the time, 'My client was attacked in the prison yard. There were no weapons involved and we hope it was picked up on CCTV cameras.' He insisted that Cocky's appeal against his Dutch prison sentence would still go ahead.

On 16 November 1999, Cocky's appeal was turned down. His lawyers insisted they would take the case to the European court of human rights.

But Cocky, who's always prided himself on keeping his operation low key, was even more upset when he found out in March 2000 that a book about his criminal career had just been published. *Cocky* (Milo Books, £14.99) spells out a lot of Warren's ducking and diving and presses home the point that the man himself has managed to hold on to most of his vast fortune. 'Cocky's not happy about the book because it winds up the British authorities who are still hunting for all his hidden cash,' says one old Merseyside associate.

The police themselves are still scratching their nuts trying to get a whiff of the really big money.

'Who fuckin' knows where he's stashed it? We reckon most of it's gone to somewhere like Dubai and from there it's in a black hole,' said one frustrated cop. Cocky was also well narked about the book describing him as being nothing more than a street-level dealer in the late Eighties, 'a nobody on the first rung of the ladder'.

Meanwhile his first big backer – 'The Banker' – was now in semi-retirement in Brussels. In early 2000, the then Home Secretary Jack Straw referred to a drugs baron who had amassed a £450 million fortune and was one of the richest people in Britain. When a friend of The Banker asked if Straw had been talking about him, he replied, 'Well, I don't think so, but I'm not sure.'

Cocky was still in possession of a fortune reckoned to be in the region of £200 million. British Customs officers and police are working with the Dutch to try and grab some of that dirty dosh but they'll be lucky if they trace a tenth of what Warren owns.

Naturally, Cocky continues to claim he was fitted up by the Customs men in tandem with the Dutch police. He also insists he only owns a couple of modest houses in Liverpool and that rumours of his incredible wealth have been greatly exaggerated.

But Cocky remains one of Britain's richest gangsters. His money is stashed in tax havens and Swiss bank accounts. He's still got a penthouse apartment in Liverpool's swanky Wapping Dock development. Then there are the office blocks he's invested in, plus those 200 properties in the north west of England, mainly let out to DSS claimants.

There's also that detached eight-bedroom mansion tucked away in Hoylake on the Wirral, outside Liverpool. Then there's the villa in Holland, a couple of casinos in Spain and a disco in Turkey.

In a nutshell, Cocky Warren virtually single-handedly turned Liverpool into the hub of the British drugs trade.

* * *

In January 2001, the cops finally had a bit of a result in their bid to nab Cocky's loot when he was forced to hand over £5 million to avoid another five years in the slammer in Holland. Cocky, now 37, was well upset when his lawyers informed him that, under Dutch law, anyone convicted of a crime and suspected of profiting from it could be forced to serve time in the nick if they couldn't prove how they got the money.

Warren handed over the cash after Customs officers travelled to Holland to give evidence to Dutch authorities. The £5 million was the largest sum ever seized in Holland. The evidence included references to four properties on Merseyside plus a large amount of dosh which briefs insist was owned by Cocky. Investigators also said he owned 270 terraced houses in the

North West of England plus other businesses spread across Europe.

The Old Bill continued to try and track down more of Cocky's fortune, although privately they admitted they don't hold out much hope. As one British Customs investigator said, 'It's a pig's ear of a system. The law as it stands favours the drug baron. We have to find the money first. Society just isn't serious about tackling hard drugs.'

And they say crime doesn't pay!

Cocky later got an extra four years on his sentence for the killing of Gema Guclu following a special Dutch prison hearing on 24 February 2001. Cocky insisted he was simply defending himself when he kicked and punched his Turkish cellmate to death. Following the sentencing, Cocky said through his brief, 'I regret the man dying but I was just defending myself.'

Following his release in 2007, Cocky was soon arrested again for conspiracy to smuggle cannabis into Jersey, and eventually sentenced to another 13 years in prison at the end of 2009. In 2013, he was ordered to pay a £198 million confiscation order or face a further 10 years in jail. Thanks to his failure to pay up, he lost his appeal and remains in prison.

Chapter 3

JOSIE DALY

Josie Daly, sharp as a knife and ten times more cunning, has been servicing punters as London's most powerful madam for almost 30 years. Today the 64-year-old brothel keeper is one of the richest women in Britain. She lives in a seven-bedroom mansion called Bunty's Corner named after her dearly departed favourite Alsatian. She's got a Roller in the driveway and her vice business has earned her more than £10 million.

Josie's palace in North London is her pride and joy. She's even spent a fortune getting artists to paint pictures of her favourite pets on to the stain-glassed porch window panes. Photos of beloved Bunty, her brother Crunchy and Sammy-poo, an Alsatian-Dalmatian cross, dominate the walls of Josie's home in Crouch End. All three of them are dead now, buried in the garden with plaques and dog statues to mark their graves.

But there's another side to Josie that's summed up by the secure iron gate arrangement halfway down the hall of her house that can be slammed shut and locked in seconds. Good security is essential in Josie's game because her team are in the habit of dropping £10,000 in cash into the house at any time of the day or night.

Josie bought the house for cash eight years ago and the first thing she did was splash out tens of thousands on building a twelve-foot-high black and gold electronic fence around the whole gaff. In the driveway her pristine white Roller lies under a tarpaulin just in case it ever gets any dust on it.

Josie's also got a few other properties scattered around town; there's a hostel in nearby Crouch End, where hookers used to stay, plus two other hotels – one in Muswell Hill and a 60-bedroom flophouse nearby which grew so tatty she had to close it down. But its value has been going up at the rate of £5,000 a week thanks to London's property boom of recent years.

One former member of her staff, a pretty brunette with long legs, reckons Josie's a brothel keeper with a heart of gold. 'She never made us feel like shit and we all knew what we were getting ourselves into. I won't hear a word against her. Josie's the tops.'

These days Josie spends a lot of her time shuffling across a thick, pink shagpile in her lounge that would put Liberace to shame. Her two beloved mutts, 11-year-old Mezchal and three-year-old Fifi love nuzzling up to their mistress. Her favourite armchair is covered in her favourite colours, black and gold. But her favourite possession is ... cash. 'I love it. I live for it. It's my life,' she says to this day.

Yet despite her millions, Josie rarely leaves the capital. She hasn't had a holiday in more than 25 years. She says she'll never leave London and it's her life. And London certainly knows Josie – especially the local cozzers and the courts of justice. Josie reckons she has a reputation to maintain and just to prove it before a recent case she bunged a mate a few bob to produce a glossy press release professing her innocence. In it she claimed that sickness had prevented her from stopping her massage parlours providing more services than British Telecom. 'When I was in good health, I stamped out any illegal activity, sacking any girls associated with it.' Really, Josie?

But then Josie's fancy mansion sitting atop Crouch End is a far cry from her humble roots in southern Ireland. Born in the village of Ardangeehy, County Cork, she was the youngest of eight children. Her parents, Jack and Eileen, ran a smallholding and struggled to feed their kids. 'We had cows and a couple of ponies, pigs and chickens,' says Josie. 'I wasn't very good at school and left at 15 with no qualifications. But when I was older I was good at whatever I did.'

That's when Josie headed across the water to stay with a sister called Margaret in Bournemouth. She became a student nurse. Then Josie, a real looker in those days, started knocking off a handsome young student doctor from Bournemouth. The couple had a daughter, Emelia Tawaih. Her only child, now in her thirties, has remained loyally by her mum's side ever since.

A few years later, Josie moved to London where she trained in tissue studies at Paddington Technical College. A spell working at a clinic that treated baldness followed. Not long after that Josie fell into the London massage parlour game. She has a rose-tinted recollection of those good old days. 'I worked at a hospital with a nice young man called John who had a woman friend called Anne who ran a massage business. We were talking about it one day and I was due some holidays so I went to help her run the place. It was very, very busy there and I was getting paid and I started saving.'

Josie ended up running that sauna for a year before branching out on her own. She even reckons she took a massage course along the way which later helped her 'spot the women coming to work for the wrong reason'.

By the early 1980s she was pulling in a small fortune. 'The clients were lovely. We'd sit and chat for hours.' Then in 1992 Josie says she suffered a massive heart attack and began taking a 'less active role' in the business which now had three 'branches' – all in the Camden area. Josie briefly owned another establishment as well before selling it on. The local cops had her labelled as 'a premiership' brothel keeper.

Josie even ran a massage training centre, which provided girls with NVQ qualifications. She also owned another house where many of the girls would stay. Josie made a crust out of that operation as well, by charging them rent.

Girls worked in Josie's four brothels around the clock on 12-hour shifts and up to one thousand geezers came through her premises each six-day week seeking out some of Josie's renowned 'extras'. Josie took a minimum £10 cut from each and every one.

The only time she had a problem with her girls was when she employed a fella in drag by mistake. 'This girl was really lovely with blonde hair and nice boobs,' she later explained. 'But I didn't realise it was a bloke waiting for a sex change until some clients rang up and told me I'd employed a man. I had to ask him to leave.'

Then in 1992 the good old *News of the Screws* took a pop at Josie and turned her over in a splash article headlined 'Cops and Brothels,' which exposed some of her most valuable customers as being ... the Old Bill! The tabloid even uncovered that Josie was employing a former CID chief to do her books. That same silly old plod had fixed up two hookers for the paper's undercover investigator posing as a punter.

The ex-cop even encouraged Josie to advertise her vice business in police magazines. The *News of the Screws* then got hold of a letter signed by him which confirmed that he had been 'a very close friend' of Josie Daly for the previous 20 years.

But then Josie always handpicked her staff and confidants with great care. Her grown-up daughter, Emelia, regularly helps out on the reception of her massage parlours. When Josie was turned over by the tabloids she even boasted to one reporter disguised as a punter, 'The police need a massage too, you know. I was even invited to a CID Christmas ball. I took a bottle of whisky and a bottle of brandy, but I didn't stay. It was too noisy for me.'

Josie, then married to a retired GP from Wolverhampton, also told the undercover hack, 'Good luck to the girls, I say. They make a fortune. I'm happy with what comes through the till. Everyone does well. Even my receptionist can earn £100 a day with tips from the girls.'

* * *

For more than 20 years Josie kept the Old Bill at arm's length thanks to greasing the right palms and making sure all the right movers and shakers got exactly what they wanted when it came to a bit of the old slap and tickle. Josie gainfully employed more than 50 women, aged between 18 and 30, many from Britain and

Eastern Europe and the Far East in her operation and she took home a fortune in anyone's terms. Josie was in the habit of dropping in unannounced at her premises in her chauffeur-driven white Roller just to make sure all the usual services were being provided.

Then the cops launched a crackdown and undercover police posing as customers were met by receptionists who handed them a menu listing a choice of sauna, steam and massage. After paying £10 or £15 to the receptionist, customers were handed a towel and invited to take a shower before being asked to choose a girl. Then a range of sexual services were offered as 'extras', costing another £15 to £50.

Josie only came unstuck when the cops discovered that some of her premises, licensed as massage and sauna parlours by the local council in Camden, didn't even have a sauna! They also reckoned she'd been hiring girls smuggled into Britain by illegal immigrant traffickers.

The boys in blue traced the ownership of the massage parlours to Josie's home in Crouch End. They watched staff pick up keys there every morning and they spotted bags of cash were taken from the premises to her mansion several times a day. Josie later admitted that there were also large sacks of rubbish deliberately dropped at the house to avoid arousing the suspicion of the local police. As DI Paul Holmes said, 'She was a significant player in the London prostitution racket.'

When Josie was finally nicked in the summer of 1999, a lot of faces reckoned she might blow the lid on some of her VIP client list which included politicians, celebrities and a bunch of top cops. Instead, Josie took to her wheelchair, admitted three counts of controlling prostitution and avoided a spell in the slammer by claiming she was at death's door. Some of Josie's rich and powerful clients even sent bouquets of flowers to Harrow Crown Court, North West London, where the case was heard. The court heard she had at least ten bank accounts. Some showed balances of up to £90,000. Another £104,500 was found in the bedroom of her prized mansion.

Josie was such a shrewd operator, however, she'd openly declared a turn-over of £250,000 for tax purposes. But as prosecutor Brendan Kelly told the court, 'This was simply a reflection of the aggregate of the receptionists' fees and made no account of the income received by the prostitutes.'

Naturally, the Old Bill insisted, 'This was a very, very profitable business. We had known about Josie Daly for some time, but didn't realise the scale of her operation.' Another policeman described her as a 'plausible raconteur' and 'a very controlling, exploitative woman'.

The court exercised its power to confiscate cash and assets amassed over the previous five years. Josie looked set to cop a figure as high as £7.5 million, based on £3 million that had been invested in property and £4.5 million that had passed through her bank accounts. But following a lengthy conflab between lawyers outside the court on the last day of her appearance, the prosecution agreed to a figure of £2 million because dear old Josie had been a good girl and paid all her VAT and income tax from her sex business. The judge even accepted that a third of her business was legit.

Giving her a year to cough up the cash or face five years inside, Judge Barrington Black said, 'The defendant has accepted she profited from the running of what has been described as a series of well-run and highly organised brothels. It is perfectly clear that the defendant was fully aware of what was going on.' But the judge wouldn't swallow Josie's supposed illness when she arrived in court in that wheelchair. He said he had 'misgivings' about her condition.

Outside the court Josie admitted that she still lived with her daughter in her £1 million mansion in Crouch End and still owned her white Roller. She also conceded that losing £2 million wouldn't make much difference to her five-star lifestyle. Josie reckoned she'd have to flog her three 'saunas' to pay the fine. But there was no way she'd part with her mansion – it was her pride and joy. There's no doubt that shrewd operator Josie still had a fortune stashed away somewhere. She also wasn't shy about mentioning that some of her best customers were members of the Met's top brass.

Irish-born and renowned for her use of the blarney, Josie told one keen young hack she'd be celebrating her escape from jail with a glass of the best champers, 'I'm glad the court allowed me to choose what properties to sell because it would have been awful to lose my house.' Josie also told anyone who would listen that she was retiring from the vice game. She insisted, 'I am afraid I will have to retire now because I can't start again. I never want to go through this again.' But as one local cop said later, 'Josie'll still have her finger in the game, if you know what I mean.'

Even Judge Barrington Black conceded, 'A woman can offer her body if she wants to. Prostitution, as we all know, has been going on forever. What the law cannot accept is that others, be they men or women, should profit by such an act.'

Josie still hoped she might get away with paying less. She said, 'I was hoping for £1 million which would have been easier to find, but I'll sort it. I don't want to go to prison. I don't think I would come out alive. As far as I'm concerned, I didn't know what the girls were up to. I was never there because of my ill-health. They did exactly what they liked.'

Throughout all this Josie continued to describe her brothels as 'highly respectable places visited by doctors, lawyers and bankers'. She added, 'We had a wide range of customers. Some of them had been coming for a long time.' Josie even made a point of saying how disgusted she was by the hundreds of used condoms found by the police when they'd raided her premises. But minutes later she boasted to one reporter, 'I know all my girls because I train them all. I like to take on girls who've never done it before. They're the best.'

By the time Josie was nicked in 1999 she'd paid off all the mortgages on at least half a dozen properties she owned and she intended to leave everything to her daughter.

In July 2000, the London *Evening Standard* splashed Josie's picture across the front page with a banner headline DOWNFALL OF THE £7 MILLION MADAM. As one of her associates later pointed out, 'Josie was laughing all the way to the bank when she read that one. She's got a fortune tucked away and they'll never find it.'

But there's another aspect to Josie's business acumen; she provided a valuable service to geezers from all walks of life. 'Josie paid her tax like any normal, law-abiding citizen but she's been punished out of all proportion to the laws she allegedly broke,' one of her former girls said after Josie was exposed in the press.

Josie always prided herself on her independence and she regularly saw off local faces who tried to muscle in on her business over the years. Josie Daly's name is well known to many of the gangsters mentioned in this book, especially the Adams family. 'But we left her alone 'cause she was a real pro and she had our respect,' says one North London face.

But now she was 'semi-retired' it was certain that ownership of her thriving business may be sold on to a team of local gangsters.

Islington Council has already granted a new licence to one of Josie's old saunas and Haringey council has received a new application to run another. Islington Council confirmed that one of the saunas, the Aqua, had been licensed to a 48-year-old builder who gave two ages and two different addresses in Companies House records.

As one of her former girls explained, 'The cops have really blown it. They've turned over Josie and forced her to retire which has meant that a heavy family from East London has now taken over what had been a well-run, crime-free business. The stupid Old Bill have created more problems than they've solved.'

No doubt the law knows full well that Josie's knocking shops are still operating. Nothing's changed except the gentle, girl-run vice world created by Josie Daly has been replaced by East Londoners hell-bent on squeezing every penny of profit out of the premises.

Chapter 4

LA PATRONA

ROYAL BELGRAVE HOUSE, VICTORIA, CENTRAL LONDON, OCTOBER 1998

Dawn was still an hour away as eight black-clad figures armed with semi-automatic shooters crept on to the roof of one of London's poshest apartment blocks. Down on the street, another team was swarming through the back door of the building.

Minutes later, the SWAT teams of armed police burst in through the front door of Colombian cocaine cartel boss Luisa Bolivar's luxury flat just as the other mob abseiled down from the roof. They were taking no chances after being warned that Luisa – known as La Patrona (Lady Boss) – kept weapons on the premises and could well be accompanied by armed minders.

Luisa Bolivar has earned millions and lived a life of luxury in London that includes that £500-a-week apartment overlooking the Thames, a driver and limo to take her to £100-a-head restaurants and all the best designer clothes stores. And it's all down to her role as chief supplier of Colombia's finest marching powder to many of the city's richest residents. This beautiful

37-year-old drug baroness is a member of one of Colombia's most powerful drug cartels. She's made a fortune running a vast network of couriers bringing Charlie into Britain.

The petite, dark-haired Latina temptress Luisa brought murder and mayhem to the streets of London when one of her fellow South Americans showed disrepect to her handsome drug baron lover. As London DS Richard Blackwell says, 'She spent her time drinking champagne in clubs. She worked for the Colombian drug cartels. If she hadn't made one stupid mistake she'd still be out there making a fortune.'

* * *

Luisa Bolivar's transformation from the prim, naive teenager who arrived in London in 1978 to a manicured, sophisticated 37-year-old drug baroness was incredible. Back in the late seventies she'd been a penniless cleaner who told everyone she'd escaped Colombia because of its drugs and violence. She married her first husband, Frank Fleming, within a short time of arriving in London and told him she wanted to be a lawyer.

Ex-husband Fleming, 55, was later stunned to find out that in five short years Luisa had risen through the ranks to become one of the most powerful Colombian cartel operators in Europe. 'When I was married to her she was pure as the driven snow.

Butter wouldn't melt in her mouth. She didn't smoke, drink or even swear. She was a real lady and had such high principles.'

Her ex-hubby also recalled, 'She told me she came here because she didn't want to live in a country with drugs, violence and killings. She hated drugs more than anything else. She had a passion against it, because she had seen what they had done to people back home. She is one of the nicest people I have met. She had perfect manners and was well-educated and bright. She was a grafter who went to bed early and got up early. It wasn't a marriage of convenience as such, but it was practical for both of us. She needed someone to look after her and I wanted the comfort. I am sure she liked the idea of being a British citizen as well.'

Luisa and her British hubby split up 15 months after the marriage. He admitted, 'I was drinking heavily and would come home late. She didn't like me doing that. I told her to leave if she wanted, so she did. We didn't keep in touch. I imagined her in a rich and successful job with a rich husband and a big house in the suburbs. I'd love to know how she went from the girl I knew to this monster. I know she wanted a better life but I can't believe she chose to get it through drugs and murder.' In fact, Luisa later married for the second time to a London-based Colombian called John Diaz and they had two children.

Luisa began her career with the coke cartels in the early Nineties when she was nicked for shoplifting in Tottenham and while awaiting trial was recruited by another inmate to work as a 'mule' for one of the cocaine gangs from her home city of Cali, the Charlie centre of the world. She was soon hiding drugs in her luggage or strapping them to her body. She proved a very cool customer and was quickly promoted. As one cop told me, 'Couriers were given £2,000 for every trip. It was a lucrative business.'

Then in 1994 Luisa was nicked with a cache of cocaine at Bogota's El Dorado airport. The couple had two daughters, now aged 18 and 13. Luisa served just nine months in prison after her coke cartel bosses were so impressed she hadn't grassed them up that they bunged the law some cash for her early release. Her two children had stayed in London with their father throughout her time behind bars.

Within days of Luisa's release she was back in London dating a debonair cartel boss called Juan-Carlos Fernandez, who went by the dual nicknames of 'Snake Hips' because of his love of dancing and 'Scarface' because of a knife attack on the streets of Cali. She'd even used her British passport gained through her first marriage to travel back to the UK. As one detective later explained, 'Things took off when she got together with Snake Hips. They were importing cocaine on a very large scale. Their income was enormous, but all illegal. She also made sure she was very hard to track down because she kept moving around.'

Luisa's work for the Cali cartel also included providing safe houses across London for illegal immigrants. But she didn't tell a soul in the capital that she'd just served time in a Colombian prison for that drug trafficking offence. Luisa remained one step ahead of the law by moving her henchmen and teams of couriers to different addresses on virtually a weekly basis.

On the surface, Luisa seemed a highly respectable member of the ever growing 60,000 official Colombian nationals living mostly in Central London. Many reckon another 20,000 are here illegally. 'And most of them are surviving by working for the drug cartels back home,' says one insider.

Many of these Colombian visitors travel into Britain as tourists and then 'disappear'. Others, as Luisa did 20 years ago, immediately seek out British men to marry. By the summer of 1996 Luisa had been promoted to recruiter and master smuggler for the Cali boys. Luisa hung out at some of the Colombian ex-pats' favourite haunts like La Bodeguita, a South American cafe in the Elephant and Castle shopping centre. It's filled with Colombian women with English surnames they've got through quick turn-round marriages.

Back in Cali, the Charlie boys elevated Luisa to the status of 'La Patrona' or 'lady boss'. She had their respect and trust and they knew the streets of London were paved in millions. Soon Luisa was raking in around £50,000 a month. She bought at least three properties in London and even splashed out £15,000 on a Harley-Davidson motorcyle for her swarthy lover's birthday.

Then she rented that five-star gaff in Royal Belgrave House, Victoria, and coughed up six months' rent (£18,000) in advance in cash. She told friends she liked living in the best part of town and was happy to pay for that privilege. The other properties she owned continued to be rented out to homeless Colombians for rip-off rents which bagged her another fortune every week. Many of them were forced to work as drugs mules in order to pay for their rent.

Luisa – who stands just a shade over five feet when not in a pair of her favourite platforms – then began throwing her dosh in the direction of a London plastic surgeon. She shelled out tens of thousands of quid on liposuction for her stomach and hips. Then she had the wrinkles removed from under her eyes and she couldn't resist some breast enlargement.

So it was that the hugely reconstructed drugs baroness known as La Patrona found herself on Friday, 8 January 1998, at her favourite bar El Barco

Latino, moored on the north side of the Thames near the Temple tube station. At one table on the crowded, floating nightclub sat 16-year-old Jorge Castillo, nick-named Little Egg because of his shaven head, and several friends. At another table, Luisa was drinking with her drugs baron Latin lover Juan-Carlos Fernandez, the man with the double-barrelled nickname Snake Hips/Scarface.

A few minutes later a muscle-bound crony of Little Egg's called Yostin Ortiz accused Fernandez of touching him up – the worst slight in the macho Latin-American underworld. A fight broke out and Little Egg stupidly ripped the £500 gold chain from Fernandez's neck and ran off. The kid had only just escaped the slums of Bogota where both his parents had been topped in a feud between rival drug gangs.

La Patrona Luisa was furious at Little Egg's 'disre-spect' to her powerful gangster lover. Fernandez drew his finger across his throat because he wanted the boy knocked off. Luisa had bought the gold chain for her steamy lover just a few days earlier. The next day she recruited hitman Hector Cedeno, 30, who'd just got back into Britain after serving time for cocaine posses-sion and grievous bodily harm in New York. Cedeno slipped into Britain after flying into France and catch-ing the Eurostar to Waterloo station. His documents weren't even checked.

Then, La Patrona called in 22-year-old Hernando Jaramillo, known as 'The Skunk' because he shaved his head with a blonde streak running down the middle resembling the tail of the animal. He was brought on board just to make sure Little Egg was taught a lesson he'd never forget. Luisa even had the scars on her lover's throat photographed so that Little Egg could be shown the picture before his own throat was squeezed. The Skunk had slipped into Britain pretending to be an asylum seeker. Back in Colombia, knocking off a street kid would hardly have warranted a police investigation so they weren't worried. Life's cheap on the streets of Cali.

Snake Hips/Scarface watched in admiration as his curvy Latin mistress organised the hit. Just hours before the killing was scheduled to take place, he slipped quietly out of Britain on a flight to Madrid, Spain.

Meanwhile Cedeno and The Skunk turned up at a south east London council flat where they knew Little Egg was staying. They asked him if he wanted to pop out with them to score some Charlie, which is the sort of thing Colombians do as frequently as the rest of us pop out for a pint. Little Egg was up for anything so he never even questioned their motives and skipped out to their waiting car, a borrowed VW Passat.

For more than an hour the three Colombians spun around the council estates of Lambeth and Brixton knocking up coke dealers, none of whom were in. Then the Passat turned into the Camberwell New Road and on to a notorious housing estate known to locals as 'Hell' where there had been a dozen shootings and at least three murders committed during the previous 12 months. They quickly scored a wrap of Charlie.

Then they parked the car up to share out the drugs. That's when ex-Colombian cop Cedeno – reputed to have knocked off dozens back home – leaned over from the back of the Passat and whipped a shoelace around the neck of Little Egg sitting in the front passenger seat. Cedeno wore white gloves as he expertly throttled the life out of the teenage tealeaf. The Skunk watched coldly and even rang La Patrona on his mobile to see if she wanted to listen to the youth take his last few breaths of life. As prosecutor Brian Altman later told the jury during a four-month trial, 'He pleaded as far as he could for his life. But he was shown no compassion.'

With the dead kid slumped on the passenger seat, the two killers drove off laughing. That's when the Skunk called Luisa back to ask if she'd like Little Egg's ear or finger to prove the job had been done. She told them to dump Little Egg somewhere her people could inspect the corpse. A few minutes later his 5ft 3in, seven-and-a-half stone body was dropped in an industrial dustbin next to a children's playground.

That night Luisa's brother Diego was despatched to look at the body in the dumpster before giving the okay for the money to be paid. Meanwhile Cedeno went home to his flat at Tyler House, on the Stockwell Park Estate, in South Lambeth. The Skunk Jaramillo lived in Union Road, Clapham, south London. The brutal drug-fuelled Colombians had hit Britain's capital city with a vengeance.

The two hitmen then got a call from Diego saying he would hand over the first instalment of £2,000 the following day at a local tube station at one o'clock. Another £2,000 would be paid within a week. Cheap by anyone's standards.

But the exchange took place right under the nose of the local cozzers who were monitoring overhanging CCTV cameras for gangs of crackheads. The three Latinos were nicked for suspected drug dealing after the suitcase was opened. They were marched down to a copshop in nearby Belgravia where they were interrogated. Then Diego called his sister Luisa to tell her what had happened. At this stage the cops had no idea they'd just nicked a bunch of killers red-handed.

Later that same day, Little Egg's battered corpse was discovered but the police still didn't know they already had the guilty men locked up. It was only after some of the victim's family flew over for Little

Egg's cremation service that the net started to close on La Patrona and her motley crew. Little Egg's Uncle Gersain gathered together some of his nephew's young London Colombian mates and urged them to take a long, hard look at their friend's battered and mutilated body as it lay in the morgue. 'I wanted to make them think what might happen to them if they didn't change their lifestyle,' Gersain later explained.

Meanwhile, killer cop The Skunk was openly bragging about his murderous habits back in Colombia where he'd killed several street children, burning them out of sewers where they lived. He also made it clear he'd plugged a young hoodlum in London as well.

Word soon reached Luisa's kid brother Diego that other Colombians were saying he played a part in the topping of Little Egg. After a couple more days young Diego spilled the beans to the Old Bill. They realised for the first time what a heavy duty case they'd stumbled upon.

Then the police SWAT team abseiled into Luisa's fancy gaff as she was leaving the premises in Royal Belgrave House to take her daughter to school. In the apartment they found £20,000 hidden in her knicker drawer. La Patrona also turned out to be a mobile phoneholic. She had eight different mobiles and was adept at answering three phones at the same time! Her phone records made very revealing reading. She was also outraged that anyone had dared to have the bottle to inform on her.

La Patrona's eventual trial at the Old Bailey's Number One court on 11 October 1999 lasted four months. In the witness box Luisa switched on the tear taps whenever she was accused of any deadly deeds. But it didn't cut much ice with the jury. And the judge told her and her hitmen, 'You all three have been convicted on compelling evidence of a cruel, cold-blooded contract killing. That youth was executed for no better reason than having the impertinence to steal a chain from Bolivar's lover's neck. You, Luisa, doubtless with Fernandez, who escaped to Spain shortly before the killing, hunted that young man down and were party to hiring two assassins to kill him in a most brutal and barbaric fashion. You showed him no mercy.'

A jury of six men and six women had deliberated over three days before reaching their unanimous guilty verdicts. The trial cost the taxpayer £2 million and Cedeno and Jaramillo were ordered to be deported. After being sentenced to life for Little Egg's murder, Luisa's lawyer said his client would appeal against her conviction.

Not surprisingly, Luisa's little bro Diego is currently in a protected witness programme living in fear that he'll be the next one to be garrotted. He currently resides in a secret address in the north of England, but the cops admit they still don't really know why he was mug enough or courageous enough to point the finger at the evil coke baroness and her hired killers.

La Patrona's 16-year-old daughter, Sandra, who now lives at her father's council flat on a South London estate, still insists to this day, 'My mother is innocent. I am not allowed to tell you the real story.'

But the murder of Little Egg – a lowly pickpocket from the slums of Bogota – may have persuaded Luisa's bosses back in Colombia that breaking into the lucrative UK cocaine market as a direct supplier of drugs rather than a wholesaler was not as easy as they thought.

The police are still anxious to speak to her lover, drugs boss Snake Hips/Scarface Fernandez, who's since disappeared into thin air.

Chapter 5

KENNY NOYE

In the underworld, certain names resonate for the sheer, stunning audacity of their crimes. They're admired by new and old gangsters, they have the bent cops in their pockets, and they live on the very edge. Meet Kenny Noye.

Kenny was – and still is – one of the most powerful and richest criminals in Britain. A genius of the underworld, handling the proceeds of huge drug deals and legendary blaggings have helped make him tens of millions of quid. He's got a string of gorgeous birds scattered around the globe and he's enjoyed a five-star lifestyle. He's also another member of that exclusive gentlemen gangsters' club, the Brink's-Mat team. It's a legendary job that links so many of the names mentioned in this book.

Yet for much of the last 25 years Kenny Noye's been in the slammer although, typically, being under lock and key hasn't stopped him from operating as a master criminal who's earned the respect of every gangster across the nation. Kenny Noye's emergence as a major player is part of recent criminal history. It's a fascinating insight into life after the Krays and the Richardsons.

* * *

Kenneth John Noye was born in Bexleyheath, Kent, on 24 May 1947. Without smog and the inner city's concrete jungles of housing developments, Bexleyheath was the new face of south east London. It had many of the area's appealing features, but few of its bad habits. And there were some traditional reminders of London life – an excellent range of boozers, chippies and pie and eel shops.

At first Kenny Noye's folks found it strange swapping their tiny terraced house in the docklands for one of the square bungalows that dominated streets such as Jenton Avenue, Bexleyheath, where the Noyes lived. Kenny's father, Jim, had become a fully-trained communications engineer while serving his country with the Navy during the Second World War. Before that he'd been a junior docker in Bermondsey.

Jim Noye went on to become a telecommunications expert at the GPO. Kenny's mum Edith was a strong, blunt-speaking lady who took her young son under her wing from an early age. She worked three nights a week as manageress of the nearby Crayford Dog Track. The Noyes were proud that they both worked. Supporting the family was all that mattered in those days. There was no question of scrounging off the state – the Noye family didn't do things that way. They looked after their own.

And young Kenny Noye certainly proved quite a handful. At just three years old he broke his nose falling out of a tree in a neighbour's garden while pinching apples. It left him with a hooter like a prize fighter. When Kenny was five, he went to the corner shop with his mum, slipped behind the counter when no one was looking, opened the cash till and helped himself. Little Kenny was only caught when his mum saw a ten bob note (50 pence) sticking out of the top of his wellington boots as they were walking out of the shop.

Schoolboy Kenny was a charming, troublesome kid. These days they'd call him hyperactive. 'He got away with a lot because he was very cheeky,' his cousin Michael Noye told me a few years back, 'but he couldn't keep out of trouble for a minute. A right handful.' Young Kenny was already boasting about what he'd do when he grew up. 'Earn lots of money,' he pledged to anyone who'd listen.

In the gritty dockland areas of south east London where Kenny's old man had grown up, petty thieves were still nicking tea chests off lorries and selling every commodity they could lay their hands on. Truck drivers were kidnapped and had their loads stolen, but no one was harmed. Everything was fair game in those days; fags, booze and clothing. Railway containers were raided at night and their contents would end up on local street markets the next day.

Crime was an escape hatch for the unemployed, many of whom were part-time villains anyway. Then, in the early Sixties, armed robbery became the most lucrative form of income. In south east London the status of blaggers put them on a par with film stars in the local community.

Meanwhile, teenage Kenny Noye was starting his criminal career. At Bexleyheath Secondary Modern he leaned on other school kids for protection money. A brief spell at printer's college followed but that soon gave way to nicking motors and scooters and selling them on to other villains in south east London and Kent.

Then Kenny got hooked up in the lorry haulage business. Soon he was making a packet handling stolen gear and even copping a few bob off the Old Bill at the same time by letting them in on a few secrets in exchange for some inside info on his rivals. Kenny called it back scratching. You scratch mine, I'll scratch your's.

Kenny married his teenage sweetheart Brenda and soon had two sons, Brett and Kevin. They moved to the peace and quiet of a village called West Kingsdown, in the Kent countryside, but still within shotgun range of his old south east London haunts. That's when Kenny decided to branch out and began fronting up cash for some daring blaggings. It was a smart move as one old lag explained, 'Kenny soon found himself handling half a dozen jobs at a time. The money was rolling in.' The beauty of Kenny's criminal career was that he rarely got his own hands dirty. He'd simply put up the finance for a job and then leave it up to his team.

By the time Kenny had turned thirty he was driving a Roller, running a fleet of fancy women and even had time to become a Mason in a cheeky bid to get closer to the police, judges and politicians who were also members. The Freemasons were a strange mob. Many saw them as a secretive organisation, but others believed they were nothing more than a discreet gentlemen's club with tens of thousands of members across Britain. How much power and influence they wield through this country's politicians and lawmakers will probably never be known. But Kenny Noye knew that being a member would certainly be good for his type of 'business'.

As one cop later explained, 'Kenny Noye cynically manoeuvred himself into the Masons as if it was the right pub for him to be seen at.' Some police members of the West London Masons lodge which Kenny joined were outraged by the presence of such a villain in their 'club'. But others saw people like Kenny as an opportunity to pick up a good informant.

Secret police records relating to Kenny's criminal career up until this stage were supplied by a police source to this author in March 2000. They show just how active Kenny already was back in those early days.

On 10 October 1981, Kenny appeared in Canterbury Crown Court for importation of a firearm, evasion of VAT, providing a counterfeit document after his arrest, making a false statement to the VAT and breaking the conditions of an earlier suspended sentence. He was very lucky to get a suspended prison sentence plus a £2,500 fine. Many believe to this day that Noye's 'friends' in the police force helped him avoid a spell inside.

Then the cops put Kenny Noye under regular surveillance in a bid to trip him up. They even carried out a few raids with search warrants on his home in West Kingsdown. A Crime Intelligence Report stated that Kenny was running a stolen motor vehicle parts ring which also involved exporting lorry equipment to Syria. He was even rumoured to have supplied some of the heavy-lifting vehicles used to construct the Thames Barrier. Kenny had a finger in a hell of a lot of pies.

Ambitious Kenny was even rather partial to using the alias of Kenneth James when he wanted to travel incognito. He also kept a luxury flat in Broomfield

Road, Bexleyheath, where neighbours spotted him in the company of some tasty-looking birds. The police soon linked Kenny to more than a dozen companies and his list of 'associates' read like a *Who's Who* of the south east London and Kent underworld. Besides his Roller, Kenny drove a Jeep and various Fords that he bought directly from Fords in Dagenham through a contact. Kenny sold them on for a fat profit.

One of Kenny's former employees at his lorry yard in West Kingsdown told the cops he was terrified of Kenny and stated that he had 'suffered violence at the hands of Noye in the past'. Even back in the early 1980s, the police reckoned Kenny was dabbling in the drug trade. One time they watched him pass over £10,000 in cash to an unnamed man in the Black Swan pub, on the Mile End Road. They had no doubt it was drug money. The same informant also told the cops that Kenny had handled the proceeds from a robbery in the Blackwall Tunnel.

The police report at the time stated, 'Noye allegedly puts up the money for organised crime, he is an associate of prominent London criminals. Noye travels to and from America and the Continent to allegedly change money.' He was certainly getting around.

The Old Bill reckoned Kenny had provided hundreds of thousands of stolen bricks for the construction of a housing estate. But when the secret police report named an MP with whom Kenny 'had a business association' it made Kenny look like an even more top-notch operator.

That report also featured Kenny's full criminal record to that time:

14.12.66 Old Street Magistrates Court. Found on enclosed premises for unlawful purposes. 12-month conditional discharge and £2.20 costs.

20.6.67 South East London Q.S. Receiving stolen vehicles. Receiving stolen property. Found on enclosed premises for unlawful purpose. Borstal Training.

20.5.75 Marlborough Street Magistrates Court. Theft of sunglasses. Assault on police. Fined £50. Ordered to pay £15 costs. Also fined £15.

21.2.77 Croydon Crown Court. Handling stolen property (five cases). Possessing document with intent to deceive. Unlawful possession of a shotgun. For all the charges Noye was fined £2,100 and ordered to pay almost £8,000 in compensation plus costs. He also got a two-year suspended prison sentence.

21.3.79 Malling Magistrates Court. Dishonestly abstracting electricity. Fined £250.

In 1982, Kenny proved he had a soft side by showing the hand of kindness to a neighbour in distress. The Noyes offered West Kingsdown greengrocer Alan Cramer their sincere condolences when his 26-year-old son was killed in a car crash on nearby Death Hill. Mr Cramer was very touched by their concern: 'They sent me a nice letter with their condolences. It was one of the first we got. They said that if there was any help we needed we only had to ask and they would help in any way they could and they didn't mean moneywise. It was a nice thought.'

Many years later Mr Cramer returned the Noyes' offer of kindness by staunchly sticking up for Kenny when he faced some major headaches with the law.

As Kenny Noye's criminal enterprises continued to expand so did his 'back scratching' with a section of the police. He and a few other faces occasionally collected 'reward money' for pointing the cozzers in the right direction. This also enabled him to keep all his own illegal activities going unhindered.

Kenny's ascendancy coincided with a complete overhaul of the gangster's biggest enemy – the Met's Flying Squad. Instead of dealing with all serious crimes, the Sweeney were ordered only to tackle armed robberies. The squad's officers formed a central robbery squad run from a co-ordinating unit at Scotland Yard with four smaller groups dotted around London.

But it was the Brink's-Mat job which really put Kenny Noye on the map – and gave him respect throughout the London underworld.

* * *

The Brink's-Mat robbery is the stuff of legends. To nick so much gold and get away with enough to set dozens of people up financially for life was a gangster's dream come true.

But the sheer size of the Brink's-Mat haul of gold bullion created a major headache for the villains involved in the raid. The gang needed a mechanism, a conduit down which the gold could travel. It had to be smelted and sold into industry before any of the dosh could be shared amongst the BM team.

Some months after the blagging, a unit of undercover cops were ordered to hide out in the 20-acre garden of Kenny's vast home, Hollywood Cottage, in West Kingsdown, and see what he was up to. One night Kenny heard some movement in the bushes and charged right in and struck out at a black-clad figure he later claimed he thought was an intruder. Kenny used all his brute strength to smash his fists into the man over and over again. Then he pulled out a blade and began to plunge it into the body of undercover detective John Fordham.

In Hollywood Cottage, Brenda Noye rushed upstairs and grabbed a shotgun from one of at least half a dozen the couple kept in their bedroom cupboard. Loading the gun as she ran, Brenda Noye and Kenny's fellow Brink's-Mat operative Brian Reader headed down the drive in the direction of where they'd heard Kenny shouting. Kenny was standing over the masked figure, his Rottweilers growling.

'Who are you?' shouted Kenny angrily. 'Who are you?'

Detective Fordham was still wearing his balaclava hood. Kenny noticed the officer's night-sight binoculars. He later claimed he thought he was dealing with a rapist or a peeping tom. Then Kenny knelt down and opened Fordham's jacket to get a closer look at the wounds he had inflicted a few moments earlier. In a much quieter voice he asked Fordham, 'What're you doing here?'

Fordham didn't answer because he was close to death. Moments later police swarmed into the grounds of Hollywood Cottage and arrested Kenny for murder.

Nearly a year later, Kenny was acquitted of murdering Detective Fordham, but the long arm of the law got its revenge when he was later banged up for nine years for his role in handling the gold bullion from the Brink's-Mat blagging that links so many of this country's big-time gangsters.

Make no mistake about it, the slammer was not the place for Kenny Noye or any major league gangster.

Prison was there to take away his liberty, to lock him up and keep him from his beloved family and away from society. But Kenny knew the first man out of the gate was the cleverest man. He left the trouble-making to other, lesser mortals.

All around him in prison were drug addicts and social misfits. He saw it as a den of vice. He watched inmates inject themselves with filthy needles. He heard the gossip about who were the 'girl-boys' and who'd just give blow jobs. None of it mattered to him because he had businesses to run. He was above the riff-raff and everyone knew it.

As one former south east London thief taker later pointed out, 'Like other parts of life there's a pecking order in prisons, and the more successful the criminal is the higher up the pecking order he will be. He'll have an easier life because he'll have gofers running around doing his chores for him.'

In 1987 – during a spell inside the relatively easy-going Swaleside Prison on Kenny's manor of Kent – Kenny met a psycho-drug peddler called Pat Tate who told him all about a new designer drug called Ecstasy, which was just starting to take off in Britain. Pat Tate convinced Kenny to invest £30,000 in one of his Ecstasy deals. Many villains reckon that it was the first of millions of pounds of Brink's-Mat cash that helped flood Britain with Ecstasy in the late 1980s and early 1990s.

(Tate, his partner Tony Tucker and another drug dealer called Craig Rolfe were later shot dead at point blank range as they sat in their Range Rover in an Essex field.)

Legend has it that Kenny made £200,000 back from that original £30,000 investment. Drugs were undoubtedly where the really big profits could be made. Blaggings would soon be a thing of the past. Like all good operators, Kenny Noye knew it was time to change direction. From inside nick, Noye invested vast sums of his considerable fortune, estimated in the late 1980s at £10 million, in the drugs explosion.

On his release from prison in 1994, Kenny decided to branch out into some high-tech villainy by joining forces with his old mate John 'Little Legs' Lloyd to form what later became known as 'The Hole-in-the-Wall Gang'. One of their members was a timid computer geek called Martin Grant who was recruited to help churn out plastic counterfeit credit cards which were then going to be used to withdraw money in one specific 24-hour period. Kenny reckoned the gang could net at least £100 million.

When Grant turned grass the police were so worried that Kenny and his team might get to him that they put him in a safe house with armed cops on patrol day and night. He was only ever moved by helicopter. Grant later explained, 'Remember, I have seen the other side of Kenny Noye not so much against me but against others who have mucked him about. Although he can be a very nice chap he is quite capable of turning into an aggressor.'

When the police finally moved in to arrest Kenny he was nowhere to be seen so they ended up nicking Little Legs and the rest of the Hole-in-the-Wall crew. Naturally, none of them were stupid enough to put the finger on Kenny. The law couldn't touch him even though they knew he was the main man behind the entire caper.

* * *

In May 1996, Kenny Noye made the biggest mistake of his life when he knifed to death motorist Stephen Cameron in a roadrage attack on the M25, just a few miles from his Kent home. Within hours of fleeing the scene, Noye was in a chopper rising above the country-side just outside Bristol to begin a two-and-a-half-year spell on the run from the police.

Back on the ground, Kenny's brand new Land Rover Discovery containing the knife he'd used to kill Stephen Cameron was being driven in a bizarre three-car convoy to Dartford, Kent, where it was scrapped by being crushed into a compressed box of jagged steel.

Kenny's role in the road-rage killing focused a lot of unwelcome attention on the south east London underworld. The police started wondering if Noye had been topped because other gangsters didn't like the extra heat they were suffering as the Old Bill frantically searched for the fugitive. Wherever Kenny Noye was in those early days after his escape, he was paying a heavy price for being linked to the Cameron killing.

As one former thief taker commented at the time, 'Kenny Noye may be a natural born criminal with a vast network of contacts, but will they keep him one step ahead of the police for ever?'

In the late summer of 1996, Kenny slipped quietly back into Britain and began moving from safe house to safe house. His impressive network of informants and contacts meant that he was safer here than in so-called unknown territory abroad. Such was his status in certain parts of Kent that he could drink and live relatively openly without the fear of being nicked. It was a measure of the power wielded by Kenny Noye.

Kenny was also taking a leaf out of his old friend John 'Little Legs' Lloyd's book. He'd done exactly the same thing when he was a supposed fugitive in America following the Brink's-Mat blagging. The nearest the cops ever really got to grabbing Kenny was in early 1997 when an anonymous tipster said that he was holed up in a small terraced house in Catford. They swooped on the house with armed officers but Kenny had long gone.

South east London criminal Gordon McFaul saw Noye in a pub in Dartford, Kent, in the spring of 1997. 'I wasn't surprised to see Kenny in the pub, he didn't have to hide. No one would grass him up,' explained McFaul. 'I had a drink with him. He seemed on good form. The bloke wasn't hiding from no one.'

Kenny was deliberately making sure he was seen out in some of his old haunts to let people on the manor know he'd done nothing wrong in his own eyes. He told anyone who would listen that he was innocent of the Cameron road-rage killing. 'But the cozzers will nail me for it anywhere. I don't stand a chance,' Kenny told one old south east London mate.

As another associate explained, 'It was important for Kenny to be seen out and about. He was tellin' his cronies that he wasn't scared of the Old Bill or no one. He was basically sayin' that if they wanted to find him they could come and try. But he had got the contacts and the knowledge to always be one step ahead of the game.'

Even Kenny Noye's cousin Michael – who'd joined him on many childhood exploits – was watched closely by the police as they desperately tried to discover where Noye had gone. 'They thought he'd get in contact with me but Kenny had more sense than to do that,' Michael Noye later told me.

In 1997, Kenny moved himself to an isolated village in southern Spain, but continued popping back and forth to south east London for important meetings despite being Britain's Public Enemy Number One. He even put up some dosh for a tasty plot to spring a drug baron from inside Whitemoor Prison, in Cambridgeshire. It involved smuggling in quantities of Semtex explosive, blasting a hole in the jail wall and then flying their man to freedom in a chopper.

One of the prison screws was nicked after an inmate leaked the escape plans to prison bosses. The man Kenny wanted to spring was an old pal serving an 18-year stretch inside Whitemoor for his part in a £65 million drug-smuggling operation. Kenny and a number of other gangsters had invested millions of pounds in this fellow's drug ring. 'Kenny needed to get the man out so they could recoup their orginal investment,' explained one source.

In November 1997, three of Noye's closest associates travelled by private plane to Spain's Costa del Sol to meet a gang of well-known drug dealers and armed robbers who agreed to acquire the Semtex and hire a helicopter. Kenny and his mates each threw in £100,000 to help finance the escape plan.

The gang had an informant who was working inside Whitemoor who'd agreed to smuggle the Semtex into the prison. It was a classic Kenny Noye-backed operation; the screw had been trapped into helping the gang because he'd been caught having it off on the sly with some bird. That same screw was already supplying many inmates with drugs inside Whitemoor.

Prison authorities foiled the escape plan just a week before it was due to happen. Kenny was spitting blood because now he knew he wouldn't get back that lost investment of several million pounds.

And Kenny's own costs for staying on the run at his Spanish hideaway were proving sky high. He was shelling out £50,000 a month to keep one step ahead of the cops. 'He was greasing palms, paying for birds, his missus, you name it. And he was having to only deal in cash otherwise the cozzers might get wind of his movements,' explained one of his old Costa del Sol mates who saw him occasionally while he was on the run.

* * *

It can now be revealed for the first time that both the British and Spanish police had Kenny in their sights months before he was finally nabbed – but no one recognised him! And Kenny's life on the run didn't stop him from earning tens of millions of pounds in drug deals from his Spanish hideaway. He even boasted that he was still paying crooked cops back home to keep him one step ahead of the law.

My enquiries show that Kenny was so heavily involved in puff smuggling that he visited Yardies in

Jamaica while he was on the run. He was even monitored by British police in Gibraltar with a local drug baron, but no one recognised him. Kenny travelled in and out of Gibraltar on a false UK passport without even having to show his photo ID and was photographed by the Spanish cozzers with a local girlfriend called Mina because she was under surveillance. But again, no one recognised him.

In Spain, Kenny bought a luxury yacht for £200,000 and chartered it out to drug smugglers. And he so terrified the owner of the house he'd bought in the tiny village of Atlanterra, that the man went into hiding in Germany after accepting Noye's cash no-questions-asked offer.

One-time volatile Kenny even pulled a knife on a middle-aged neighbour in Atlanterra when the man climbed over Noye's gate to talk to his gardener. Frequently Kenny secretly smuggled his father, wife Brenda and other relatives and mates to his home in Spain even though the Old Bill in Kent were supposed to be shadowing their every move. And Kenny wasn't even spotted when twenty Spanish cops patrolled the next-door house because one of Spain's senior politicians spent the summer at the property.

But even Kenny Noye can be taken to the cleaners occasionally; in Spain he was conned by a local so-called property developer into investing £100,000 into the renovation of a local hotel which never happened. Throughout his stay in Spain, Kenny flew various mistresses out to Portugal then smuggled them across the border and rented them isolated houses at least ten miles from his own home.

Yet he continued travelling extensively from his Spanish hideout. His false passport contained numerous stamps showing that he had been a regular visitor to Jamaica and Morocco. One Noye associate explained, 'Kenny was up to all sorts of deals. He went to the home of a British villain living in Morocco and they set up a smuggling operation together. Then he linked up with a West Indian he'd been inside Swaleside Prison with and they met some seriously heavy Yardies in Jamaica.'

In mid-June 1998, the police back in Kent had a lucky break when they got a call from a long-time informant who gave them the mobile phone number of another villain who was in regular contact with Kenny Noye. When the grass demanded a £100,000 tip-off fee if it led detectives to Noye, the cops started to take him very seriously.

Kent Plod immediately requested assistance from MI5, who sanctioned round-the-clock surveillance of the target's phone from their headquarters overlooking Vauxhall Bridge in London. MI5 – Britain's domestic security service – had some really tasty surveillance equipment and had been helping police across the country with their enquiries since the mid-1990s.

By the end of August 1998, Kenny had been traced to his house in the tiny Spanish seaside village of Atlanterra, just south of the city of Cadiz. Days later he was arrested in a nearby restaurant by Spanish and Kent cops and slung in a shithole jail in Cadiz. His gorgeous brunette girlfriend disappeared into thin air before the cops could find her.

Even while awaiting extradition from jail in Spain Kenny flirted with a tasty female prison officer in custody in Cadiz. Prison source Oscar Labato later explained, 'Noye was only in that prison a few days when a male officer noticed that he was spending increasing amounts of time talking to this particular woman officer. She was immediately transferred to another wing of the prison.' Just a couple of months later the same woman screw was fired for having sex with an ETA terrorist inmate. She was later reinstated after claiming unfair dismissal even though she admitted having an affair with an inmate. She has never revealed exactly what happened with Noye.

Kenny's team of highly paid Spanish briefs reckoned he stood a good chance of avoiding extradition. But in March 1999, a bunch of Madrid judges threw out all his appeals and Kenny knew he'd be heading home within a few weeks.

Back in Britain, the tabloids revealed that Kenny's missus Brenda was having a romance with a Cornish fisherman. Some cops reckoned the article had been deliberately fed to Fleet Street to make it clear Brenda Noye was no longer married to Kenny. One Kent police contact explained, 'It makes Noye look more like the victim rather than the perpertrator. It also makes Brenda a hostile witness. In other words, she can't testify against him.'

Finally, on 20 May 1999 – after a couple of last ditch appeals by Kenny's briefs had failed – Kenny was handcuffed and ordered out of his cell at Madrid's Valdemoro Jail. Then he was bundled into an anonymous white van escorted by two plain Seat saloons out towards the city suburbs. Less than thirty minutes later Noye was handed over to three Kent policemen at Madrid Airport and secretly flown to London's Gatwick Airport.

The following day, 21 May, Kenny appeared before magistrates in his old manor of Dartford to hear the murder charges concerning the death of Stephen Cameron. Kenny was immediately taken to the most secure prison in London – Belmarsh – and placed in solitary confinement at his own request.

Back in England, the London underworld was buzzing with rumours about who'd grassed up Kenny Noye. Stories were circulating that the informant had qualified for £100,000 reward money ... but would he live long enough to enjoy it? As one criminal source said at the time, 'I can tell you there'll be an even bigger price on that bastard's head for turnin' in Kenny Noye.'

Once in Belmarsh high-security jail, Kenny lorded it over his entire wing and greeted various south east London screws like they were long-lost old friends. One fellow Belmarsh inmate told me in a series of tape-recorded telephone interviews, 'Kenny Noye was the king inside here. He knew many of the staff and inmates already from when he previously served time. Some of them even knew him from his days as a petty villain in south east London and Kent. It was like home from home for him. The staff said he'd been given his own wing at Belmarsh for his own protection but his guys in the main part of the prison said that Kenny had requested to be isolated because he hoped he could secretly carry on running all his rackets without interruption.'

Kenny even got people inside Belmarsh to run errands for him and there were rumours that he had a mobile phone with him at all times. 'Noye had his own team of cronies in the main part of the prison,' explained my man in Belmarsh. 'It's all a game to Noye. Prison doesn't stop him operating. It's just an inconvenience.'

Kenny even let it be known that he was so confident he'd be acquitted of the murder of Stephen Cameron that he'd authorised his sidekick in Spain to get his house ready for his return. He even bunged thousands to his builder back in Spain from his prison cell. 'He was that confident he'd get off. His cronies were spreading the gospel according to Noye around the entire prison. It's a game that Noye is very good at,' added the inmate.

In November 1999, I was approached by a Kenny Noye contact and asked if I wanted to meet one of the money men who had known all about Kenny's movements while he'd been on the run. The meeting was to take place in a hotel bar to the west of London and, my contact warned me, 'This geezer will get up and walk away if you try and ask him anything directly about Kenny Noye.'

The man who showed up spent the following three hours telling me in great detail about most of Noye's movements during his two and a half years on the run. And when it came to explaining why many other criminals wanted to bring Noye's flight from justice to an end, this fellow said, 'It was time for the cozzers to haul Kenny in. He knew they'd catch up with him in the end.'

* * *

All the gossip and rumours surrounding the so-called roadrage killing of Stephen Cameron were finally put to rest when Kenny Noye walked into the number two court of the Old Bailey on Thursday, 30 March 2000 – nearly four years after that murder on the M25. Gone was the confident swagger that had accompanied Kenny's last appearance in the very same dock of the very same building 14 years earlier. This time Kenny, now grey-haired and dressed in a grey cardigan, sat hunched almost like an old man in the dock between three prison officers. His eyes panned the jury of eight women and four men from the moment he was led in by three prison screws.

Before the case could proceed, the judge Mr Justice Latham ordered round-the-clock protection for each juror. He even told them all, 'There are many people who have an interest in this case and its outcome. I have arranged for you to be provided with escorts that will, I am afraid, affect your daily life to some extent.'

Kenny claimed he was simply defending himself when he pulled a knife out from under the front seat of his car and stabbed Cameron to death on the M25 roundabout. But the jury didn't believe him and found him guilty of murder by a verict of 11-1.

Kenny let out a deep gasp and held his head in his hands when he heard the verdict. Victim Stephen Cameron's father leapt from his seat just feet away, hands aloft in celebration and shouted, 'Yes.'

Then Mr Justice Latham told Kenny, 'The jury having found you guilty of murder, there is only one sentence I can impose and that is one of life imprisonment.' Kenny looked unsteady on his feet as the three screws led him down the 21 steps from the dock of number two court to the cells below. A few minutes later a van, its siren blaring, took him back to Belmarsh.

Outside the court DS Dennis McGookin, the Kent officer who led the last two years of the road-rage investigation, said, 'He's an evil man. He's been jailed for life and that's where he should remain.'

After the verdict, the son of Kenny's earlier 'victim', DC John Fordham, broke his family's 15-year silence on Kenny. 'You make your own tomorrows and I think he has made his. You can't go on committing crimes,' said John Fordham. 'I am very pleased for the Cameron family, very pleased with the verdict. But it doesn't bring my dad back.'

In the hours following the verdict, it emerged that Kenny's defence, estimated to have cost between £500,000 and £1 million, had been funded by the taxpayer. He'd been granted legal aid because on paper he was not worth a penny.

Meanwhile, Kenny Noye's criminal status as Public Enemy Number One would ensure he received the utmost respect from staff and inmates at whatever prison he ended up in. As one policeman pointed out, 'This isn't the last we shall hear of Kenny Noye.'

And there was no doubt Kenny's crime empire would continue to expand, even from inside prison. South east London face Gordon McFaul reckons, 'Noye's addicted to crime. Nothing stops him. His reputation as a master criminal is second to none. If it wasn't for his filthy temper the rest of the world wouldn't even know who he was.'

In the late summer of 2000, Kenny even pocketed half a million quid from the sale of his luxurious Spanish home – and authorities couldn't touch a penny of it! Kenny got top dollar for the gaff by pouring £30,000 into improvements despite being in the slammer for the previous two years.

He even splashed out hundreds of pounds on getting special glossy sales brochures with photos circulated amongst his criminal associates in a bid to sell the house. 'Noye continues to operate even from a prison cell. It's outrageous,' said one of his neighbours in Spain, Hermann Ritz. 'He behaves more like a property developer than a convicted murderer.'

Kenny believes that despite a pledge from authorities to seize all his assets, they will be powerless to grab the proceeds from the house sale because, in legal terms, he never actually owned the property. It was never registered in his name.

'Kenny's been buying and selling property like this for years in other people's names,' explained one source in south east London. 'He used to do it to avoid paying taxes but it's come in even more handy now that everyone's after his dosh.'

Kenny even threw in his beloved £20,000 blue Shogun jeep for good measure. Added his associate, 'Kenny really thought he'd be acquitted over the M25 killing and would return here to live out the rest of his days, so when he got the life sentence the first thing he did was ensure the house was sold.'

Kenny Noye is supposed to be one of the Home Secretary's biggest targets in his bid to confiscate money and property from Britain's gangsters. But he still currently owns at least SIX properties around the world worth at least TWO MILLION POUNDS. 'Kenny's laughin' really. He knows that no one can touch those properties abroad and he's made sure that everythin' he's financed in Britain is in other people's names,' explained one underworld source. 'You could call it Kenny's pension policy. He reckons he'll be out of prison one day and he wants to make sure he doesn't have to struggle.'

Kenny still currently owns a share in a hotel in Spain, a timeshare holiday complex in Northern Cyprus, two penthouse apartments in a nearby town in Cyprus. His wife lives in a detached bungalow in Looe, Cornwall. His parents live in a recently built detached five-bed house on his old manor of West Kingsdown,

Kent. Then there's the semi in Bexleyheath which he has in the past used to 'entertain' his mates.

In recent years, Kenny has also liquidated other assets including a fitness club in Dartford, Kent, sold for £150,000, the family home near Sevenoaks sold in 1998 for £500,000, an interest in a south east London winebar for £200,000 plus an interest in two boutiques in south east London sold for £300,000. Kenny is also believed to have retained part, if not whole, ownership of at least some of his former homes which were 'sold' for knockdown prices to criminal associates.

It's all a long way from the modest three-bed bungalow in Jenton Avenue, Bexleyheath, where Kenny was born and bred. Explained another of his criminal associates, 'Kenny Noye would have made a brilliant legitimate businessman but he couldn't resist the thrill of being a gangster.'

Kenny – the master manipulator – is currently locked up in top security Whitemoor Prison plotting his next move. Underworld sources initially believed that Kenny would name some top faces to the police in exchange for a reduced sentence. But then the key witness against him during the Cameron murder trial was gunned down by a hitman outside a shopping centre in Kent in the late summer of 2000. The murdered witness's wife told newspapers she did not believe her husband had told the truth during Kenny's

Old Bailey trial. Shortly afterwards, Kenny's legal team announced they were putting together a serious appeal against his murder conviction.

But in October 2001 the high court quashed this appeal. Despite this 'setback', this certainly isn't the last we shall hear of Kenny Noye – Gangster Number One. He's already pledged to continue his appeal through the European Court of Human Rights. If there's a way out of doing his bird, Kenny Noye will find it.

At the time of writing, Kenny Noye was still on the inside but now spending his days at HMP Standford Hill, an open prison on the Isle of Sheppey in Kent, not far from his old manor.

Chapter 6

RODDY McLEAN

Roddy McLean, big-time Scottish drug baron and alleged part-time police informant, is a man not to be crossed. A couple of years back one national tabloid featured him in its 'rich list' with a net worth of around £4.5 million. Roddy wasn't happy because he knew that sort of publicity could cause him a bucket-load of heat.

But since then it's reckoned Roddy has more than doubled his fortune thanks to some shrewd property sales and an eye for the big deal that puts most of his rivals north of the border in the shade. Roddy, now 56, owns property worth more than £1 million, plus land at Edinburgh's South Queensferry and a number of boats. So he was mighty relieved when he was forced to hand over just £100,000 compensation after a recent run-in with the law. It barely made a dent in his wallet.

At one time Roddy bought one of his drug smuggling boats from Customs for a cut-price deal. The *Sea Ranger V* offshore supply vessel and its multi-million-pound cargo had been confiscated when its captain was arrested back in 1993. Months later Roddy paid £5,000 cash for the boat, even though it had a resale value of around half a million quid.

Later Customs officers claimed they'd given the boat to Roddy for a knockdown price because he was one of their most important informants – a claim that he has always strenuously denied. Anyway, Roddy immediately renamed the 150ft vessel the *Toto* before registering it in Belize and then transporting it from Leith in Scotland to a South African shipping agent for leasing. Many believe it was used many times to transport puff into Scotland.

Back on the mainland, the police eventually launched Operation Balvenie specifically to try and net Roddy. For almost a year they seemed to be getting nowhere fast. It was as if Roddy knew exactly what they were up to. Maybe he had 'a few friends on the force', so to speak. The cops dug into every aspect of Roddy McLean's lifestyle and he came up smelling of roses. He was shadowed everywhere he went. Ironically it was only when Roddy tried to give the Old Bill the slip that they stumbled on the fact he was setting up a huge drugs deal.

One day in May 1996, Roddy sauntered into Waverly Station in Edinburgh, cool as a cucumber, to catch a train to London. Customs officers were waiting for him and tailed him to a meeting with a fellow they later tagged as Brian Silverman, a link man with the Adams family, down in North London. Roddy was so obsessed with losing his shadows that he completely changed his travel plans on the journey back to Scotland. But the boys in blue had already spotted his link with Silverman.

Then a month later, Roddy was eyeballed by Customs investigators boarding another train from Edinburgh to King's Cross, in London. This time Customs officers managed to shoot some good-quality video camera footage of their subject talking to Silverman again. They knew something was about to go down.

On 11 June 1996, Customs men followed Roddy, his son Roderick Jnr and another associate as they travelled to Milford Haven, Wales, where they purchased a former lifeboat called the *Ocean Jubilee*. Roddy handed over £29,000 cash for the vessel in a plastic carrier bag. Then he and the others sailed the boat back up to Scotland. On 20 June they arrived in Scrabster Harbour on the northern tip of the Scottish mainland, claiming the boat had developed gearbox problems. They moored the boat and scarpered in a car back to Edinburgh. That's when Customs officers decided to call in the cavalry in the shape of MI5 and their high-tech surveillance equipment.

Customs soon intercepted a mobile telephone call from a shop in Roddy's home town of Edinburgh to one of Spain's major puff operators, a fellow known only as Alf. That call convinced the Old Bill that Roddy and his merry men were about to pull off one of the deals of the century.

The spooks at MI5 then firmed up that Alf had used the same phone to call another number in Holland, which turned out to be the home of a well-known puff smuggler. That link between the shopkeeper and Roddy didn't do the flashy Scottish gangster any favours at all.

Another flurry of calls between Roddy and Alf in Spain followed. Then Roddy called his man in Holland and announced the puff deal was green for go. What Roddy didn't realise was that the flying Dutchman's boat – called the *Issolda* – was about to be tracked by two spy planes packed with state-of-the-art surveillance equipment.

On the evening of 26 July, Roddy sailed off in the *Ocean Jubilee* to a spot 90 miles off the Caithness coast. The *Issolda* soon showed up bobbing on the horizon. Roddy spoke to his Dutch counterpart using the codename Popeye. At 3:24am that morning the operation to hand over the three tons of puff began. Just as the loading had finished and the boats were drifting apart, Customs cutters moved in to intercept and board both vessels. The game was up. Sadly, during the operation, Customs officer Alastair Souter died when he was crushed between Roddy's boat and a Customs vessel.

Roddy was nicked for masterminding an attempt to smuggle three tons of puff into Scotland. One of his houses was swiftly sold shortly after his arrest while his wife Susan continued living in the family's other mansion in nearby Boswall Road. Yet, as if to prove to the world he was just a hapless villain, filthy rich Roddy McLean was given legal aid to fight the impending court case. Roddy claimed he had no other way of paying for his legal bills.

When the case finally got to the High Court in Edinburgh, fifteen armed coppers with drawn semi-automatic rifles surrounded the High Court and Parliament Square in the Scottish capital while Roddy and his mates stood trial. In court, Roddy Snr admitted smuggling the three tons of puff from Morocco while everyone else denied the charges. The trial was told how Customs men pounced on Roddy's boat the *Ocean Jubilee* just after the shipment of puff had been handed over on the high seas from that Dutch yacht.

But Roddy's brief Neil Murray QC claimed in court that his client was in serious debt through his shipping business and had got involved in the drugs operation to clear those debts. 'There is no doubt in my mind that the death of Mr Souter weighs very heavily on his conscience,' said the QC, referring to the death of the Customs officer.

But the judge Lord Dawson told the court, 'The volumes involved were truly in the major league; some £3 million would have been required to purchase such a vast consignment. The profits to be made were astronomical; the retail value of these drugs being estimated at more than £10 million.'

Roddy's mate Brian Silverman's links to the Adams family back in London were disclosed in open court, even though Silverman insisted he was not a major player in the drug smuggling operation. After Silverman had given evidence, Lord Dawson told him, 'You attempted to play the part of a likeable East End rogue in order to try and hoodwink what you obviously regarded as a susceptible provincial jury. You were clearly in charge of the London side of operations and a major character in the plot.' As he was sentenced to 14 years, Silverman tried to shout down the judge. He screamed, 'I think Judge Jeffries, the hanging judge, would have been proud of you 200 years ago. This trial is going to come back and haunt you.'

Then Lord Dawson had a poke at Roddy, 'You put this deadly plan into operation, endangering the lives of a number of officers bravely doing their duty and caused the death of one such officer.'

Roddy was upset, but not that surprised, when he copped a heavyweight 28-year sentence. Seven others, including Roddy's kid, Roddy Jnr, were sent to jail for 12 years for their part in the smuggling operation. Roddy McLean and his associates have always believed they were hammered by the judge in the trial because of the 'accidental' death of Customs officer Alastair Souter. Roddy's son blew a kiss to the public gallery as he was sentenced and he raised his fist and shouted 'freedom' to the amusement of a dozen spectators.

Then the Old Bill really put the boot in by claiming Roddy had been so helpful to them that they'd turned a blind eye to many of his 'other activities' in Edinburgh. Labelling him a grass was as good as sentencing him to death. Others were quick to rush to Roddy's defence. One former associate insisted, 'That's a load of old bollocks. The coppers are just pissed off because neither Roddy nor his kid would grass anyone up. Do you think they would have got such heavy sentences if they'd been informing? Come off it!'

After sentencing, Roddy conveniently found himself sharing a cell with his son Roddy. Inside jail, screws uncovered a plot to kill the McLeans and made a point of letting the local press know they were 'taking the threats very seriously'. There was talk of a £7,500 payment being made to a hitman to plug Roddy Snr and another £5,000 to have his kid topped. Roddy later claimed the stories were put about by the police in order to pile pressure on the McLean family.

Prison staff privately admitted they thought the sentencing on McLean was 'pretty over the top considering he was only importing cannabis which half the staff and inmates in here like to smoke'.

In May 1999, Roddy McLean and his other major partner in crime had their jail sentences cut by seven years from 28 to 21 after lawyers acting for him accused his original trial judge, Lord Dawson, of adding to their sentence because of that Customs officer's death, even though nobody was found culpable of his homicide. A further two years was cut from McLean's sentence because he also happened to be a first time offender.

* * *

McLean met a frankly bizarre end in 2004, when, having absconded from the open prison he was being held in two months before, he was found dead, and partly decomposed, at a bed-and-breakfast in south London. It had been thought that he might have used his money and fled somewhere in the sun for a quiet retirement, but in death he managed to raise even more questions than he had in his extraordinary life.

Chapter 7

LITTLE LEGS

John 'Little Legs' Lloyd is a legend in his own lifetime. And his fame in the London underworld doesn't just come from having been one of the original six Brink's-Mat bullion robbers who was never brought to justice. 'This guy is deeply respected everywhere,' says one old south east London blagger. 'He's the tops.'

Little Legs, now 61, is especially revered on his old manor of the East End where he grew up. He helped plan and carry out the Brink's-Mat job and copped around £5 million in the process. The Old Bill knew only too well that Little Legs and Kenny Noye went back a long way. Kenny even flogged him one of his old houses in West Kingsdown, Kent, which Legs' partner still lives in to this day. However, shortly after his old mate Kenny was nicked for handling the gold from the Brink's-Mat bullion raid, Little Legs sensibly did a runner.

The police told everyone he'd scarpered to America. In fact, Little Legs was popping back and forth to his old London and Kent haunts completely unbothered by the so-called worldwide manhunt in his name. He even boasted to one associate that he preferred flying back to London with British Airways, 'Cos they've got a better safety record than all the other airlines.'

In the US, a Miami court ordered Legs in his absence to pay $400 million to Brink's-Mat insurers but he never coughed up a penny in Florida. Little Legs later described the court's decision as 'a fuckin' joke'.

As London's gangsters know only too well, Little Legs – nicknamed because of his spindly legs – has been a prime mover in many of the best-known blaggings of the last 30 years. His personal fortune probably tops the £10 million mark thanks to some shrewd investments of dirty money in a number of legitimate interests, including a transport business. At one stage, Legs also owned a car hire business in Kent. He was also a regular visitor to Clarke's Peacock Gym, in Canning Town, as well as often dropping in to his beloved Lovatt pub in the East End, for a swift pint.

While 'on the run' in the US, Little Legs even had his shorts specially tailored so they flattered his funny old pins. He also splashed out a few thousand bucks on some surgery to correct his disfigured toes. Back in London, a warrant was also issued for Legs' arrest in connection with Brink's-Mat and a £10,000 reward was offered. Legs' beloved common-law wife Jean Savage even copped a five-year sentence for conspiracy in connection with the Brink's-Mat raid. But more about the loyal and wonderful Jean later …

Then, in 1994, Little Legs was named on the TV crime show *America's Most Wanted*. A couple of weeks later Legs took the biggest gamble of his life by walking into Rochester Row police station with his brief to give himself up. The Crown Prosecution Service eventually ruled that there was insufficient evidence linking him to the Brink's-Mat job. The gamble had paid off.

Less than a year later, Legs reluctantly donated a five-figure sum to a consortium of insurance companies after he was fingered for his role in the 1983 robbery even though there wasn't enough evidence to prosecute him in a court of law.

But gangsters like Little Legs Lloyd can't stay out of trouble for long. Soon he'd hooked up with some of his old Brink's-Mat mates for a caper they believed would top any other crime ever committed in Britain before.

At a pub just off the Old Kent Road, a small and dirty enough place to keep most ordinary punters out, and therefore chosen for its privacy by a number of south east London faces, Legs met up with Kenny Noye and some other familiar faces. Lloyd told his mates he was planning a cash card cloning scheme he believed could net them as much as £100 million.

Cash dispensers were the key to this daring crime and Lloyd needed some backers to come in with him. Kenny Noye immediately volunteered for a piece of the action for what was to become known as 'The Hole-in-the-Wall job'(also known as the ATM scam).

Noye and Lloyd put up some hefty finance to support the team of villains who would be spending months planning the crime. Then they used their own contacts in the nick to scout around for some technical recruits to the team. The idea was to tap into the latest banking technology and an army of corrupt communications engineers and computer experts had to be recruited to make vast numbers of cloned cashpoint cards. These would then be used to empty cash from the bank accounts of thousands of ordinary people. If they pulled it off it would throw the British banking system into total chaos.

Eventually, computer boffin Martin Grant was hired from inside Blantyre House open prison in Kent. He'd been jailed for attempting to murder his wife and child but in the slammer he'd studied for a degree in electronic communications. Grant was out on day-release for work experience at a van hire business owned by Paul Kidd, another villain involved in the cashcard cloning scheme with Little Legs.

Legs and his Hole-in-the-Wall gang planned to enter British Telecom exchanges with their team of corrupt engineers to put telephone taps on the lines and memory boards. The info would then be transferred to the gang's computer. But unknown to the gang, computer nerd Martin Grant, completely out of his depth with this team of pros, was already feeding information about the credit card scam to the law. He'd confessed to a prison chaplain about the planned robbery and later made a statement of over 300 pages to the Old Bill.

Later Grant provided a fascinating insight into Little Legs Lloyd and his mate Kenny Noye. 'Noye and Lloyd were just names to me at first. They meant nothing. But people inside prison talked about them as if they were gods.' Grant said he attended one meeting with the gang where Kenny and Legs produced prison paperwork on his (Grant's) record and family background which clearly had been given to Legs by prison staff. Those details included the addresses of Grant's mother and brother.

Then, in a chilling incident, Little Legs drove Grant up to his mother's house in the Midlands and walked him through the front door and even introduced himself to Grant's mother 'just to let me know he knew where she lived'. Grant later explained, 'John Lloyd then phoned Kenny Noye to say he had met my mum. I was so scared.'

Grant added, 'Kenny Noye and Lloyd told stories about hijacking vehicles in the early days and what they did to people who crossed them.' Grant said they also made continual references to other criminal associates in Spain and the United States.

Grant says that Kenny Noye and Little Legs became very threatening towards him once they began suspecting he might be grassing them up. 'One time they got a bunch of other villains to follow me back to prison to make sure I wasn't in touch with the police,' he said. Grant also recalled an incident when Noye and Lloyd almost came to blows after they had a problem with the computers they were using as part of the scam. 'I saw Noye lose his temper with Lloyd and it wasn't a pleasant sight,' is all he'll say to this day.

After the arrest of the Hole-in-the-Wall suspects, Martin Grant was put into police custody away from prison for his own protection. Detectives were so worried that Kenny Noye and Little Legs might harm Grant they put him in a safe house with armed officers 24 hours a day and only moved him by helicopter.

Grant is still worried about Little Legs to this day: 'I know he holds a grudge against me and I'm very nervous about it.'

After Little Legs copped a five-year stretch for his part in the Hole-in-the-Wall scam, I paid his lady Jean Savage a visit at their immaculate bungalow in West Kingsdown. It just so happens that they'd bought it off Kenny Noye more than a dozen years back. Jean was a charming woman, but her Rottweilers and seven-foot-high brick wall complete with electronically controlled gates were not so welcoming.

After a ten-minute chat on her CCTV I realised she wasn't going to let me in for a chat about Little Legs and his antics. In 1999, Legs was released from prison and nothing has been heard from him since.

'But he's around and he's looking for new business opportunities – or so I've heard,' one old south east London face told me recently.

Chapter 8

GOLDFINGER

The long arm of the law finally caught up with John 'Goldfinger' Palmer at the Old Bailey in May 2001, when he copped an eight-year stretch. Over more than thirty years he'd earned literally hundreds of millions of pounds from his role as the most shadowy so-called businessman in Britain.

Palmer became this nation's wealthiest prison inmate when he was jailed for operating the world's largest timeshare fraud. But that prosecution barely scraped the surface of his criminal enterprises which elevated him to the position of 105th wealthiest person in Britain, according to one published 'league table' in 2000. His nickname 'Goldfinger' came from when he was accused, and found not guilty, of handling the bullion from, yes you've guessed it, the Brink's-Mat robbery near Heathrow Airport in 1983.

The 51-year-old villain looked stunned as the Old Bailey jury delivered its guilty verdict after nearly six weeks of deliberation. You see, John Palmer considered himself to be untouchable and he so nearly got away with all of it.

In the dock that day, tough guy Palmer went a whiter shade of pale and was close to tears as he slowly took off his £10,000 Cartier wristwatch and handed it to his brief before being led away to the cells. Before disappearing, Palmer glanced across at Christina Ketley, his business partner and mother of their ten-year-old son. She was also convicted of involvement in the same fraud. (He's also got a wife and two daughters in the West Country.) Ketley, 37, was given a suspended sentence. The jury later threw out charges against Palmer's nephew, Andrew Palmer, aged 37.

Earlier in the proceedings, John Palmer even conceded to the court, 'I acknowledge I have a strong, dominant personality, probably from my background. I have always relied on my wits for the benefit of those near and dear to me.'

Over the previous eight months, the Old Bailey had heard evidence from several of the almost 20,000 mainly British couples who had been duped out of their life savings by Palmer's outrageous time-share antics in Tenerife. It's reckoned his victims lost more than £30 million. The investigation into Palmer's activities and the eight-month trial (plus an earlier abandoned hearing) cost at least £15 million of public money.

Yet Palmer had been so supremely confident of once again escaping conviction he even defended himself in court. He was described by prosecutor David Farrer, QC, as 'the largest shark in the time-share water'. He treated his victims like 'a bunch of mugs'. They ranged across the social spectrum from barristers to pensioners, with the elderly forming the bulk of his long line of 'mugs'.

A procession of senior police officers gave damning evidence against Palmer. Detective Roy Ramm, a former commander at Scotland Yard heavily involved with the prosecution of the Brink's-Mat gang, denounced him as 'a serious organised criminal'. But John Palmer wouldn't stand for that kind of allegation; he immediately accused Ramm and many of his colleagues of corruption.

Palmer and Ramm then glowered at each other as Ramm told the court how Palmer had been taped by TV reporters on *The Cook Programme* offering to launder £60 million worth of drugs money. A furious Palmer hit back by insisting that Ramm and his colleagues illegally lined their pockets with reward money from the loss adjusters involved in tracking down the Brink's-Mat gold. Each time Palmer accused Ramm of corruption, the ex-detective threw back at him the drug money allegations.

Palmer even suggested that the taxpayers could have been spared the expense of a costly trial if authorities had instead sued him. He proudly mentioned that he could easily have afforded a £50 million loss in that department.

'You don't know how rich I am,' he sneered at Roy Ramm. 'Were you aware of my private plane, and my two helicopters?' he asked, pausing for the Old Bailey jury to savour his performance.

But then John Palmer was mighty proud of his 'achievements'; he employed 3,000 people to run his timeshare empire. There were also the three pilots for his Lear jet which remained constantly on standby at an airport on the outskirts of London throughout his trial. There was also a six-man crew for his £6 million yacht, *Brave Goose of Essex*, plus the liveried chauffeur who drove him to court each morning. Not to mention gourmet cooks, butlers, landscape gardeners and numerous others at his various properties across the world. They included a converted coach house at Battlefields, near Bath, a huge villa in Tenerife complete with a pool stocked with rare albino frogs and a château in Caen, France, with two golf courses.

No wonder John Palmer was at the time of his trial in 2001 reputed to spend more than £1 million a year on a team of crack bodyguards, including a number of former SAS soldiers. 'This is a villain with enemies on both sides of the fence,' says one south east London criminal, who's had dealings with Palmer in the past.

Palmer's timeshare developments include the Royal Gardens and Flamingo Park in Tenerife. He also owned Harleys nightclub in nearby Playa del las Americas plus other hotels, amusement arcades and bowling alleys – all of them perfectly respectable places.

'Not bad for a scrap metal seller,' he proudly told the jury during his 2001 trial.

Palmer's original hearing on the same timeshare charges began in September 1999 but was abandoned after eight months because he successfully argued that adverse press publicity connecting him to his mate Kenneth Noye had prevented him from getting a fair trial.

The retrial kicked off on 2 October 2000. Palmer opened his case by declaring to the jury, 'I have been portrayed as a gangster. I am not a gangster nor ever have been a gangster.'

During the trial, Judge Gerald Gordon had to intervene several times after Palmer began shouting and finger jabbing at police witnesses. While Palmer admitted to the jury that a fraud had taken place he insisted it had all gone on behind his back.

Palmer also claimed that his lover Christine Ketley, was innocent of any involvement. The jury then heard how Palmer had doubled her salary after they became lovers. He even appointed her head of one of his companies, Island Financial Services. Prime operator

Palmer was so confident of walking free from the Old Bailey that he proudly showed prosecutors brochures of a £10 million leisure complex and a £40 million hotel that were still under construction in Tenerife.

Ironically, it's reckoned that much of Palmer's so-called business empire survived his incarceration as he had a team of trusted lieutenants running it. An army of lawyers and accountants helped offset most of his companies so that little of his fortune could be touched while he was in jail.

And just like his friend Noye, he thrived despite being behind bars. 'It was a major inconvenience but he hardly went broke as a result of that court case,' said one of his oldest associates. Rumours that Palmer enjoyed a prime job in prison which gave him virtually unhindered use of a private phone have never been denied by jail authorities.

* * *

Until his conviction at the Old Bailey, John Palmer had bathed in the glory of a long criminal career that helped make him one of the richest, most feared, yet secretive gangsters in Britain over the past thirty years.

One of seven children, he grew up in dismal poverty near Birmingham where he swindled mates and associates out of cash when they all worked together in market stalls in the suburb of Solihull. Palmer bristled with pride whenever he told how, despite being a dyslexic who left school at 15, he had made it to the top. Some of his pals from the old days say he never completely learned how to read and write. After leaving school, Palmer joined his brother in a roof-tiling business, then went on to become a door-to-door salesman offering paraffin at knockdown prices.

One of his earliest clashes with the police was in 1973 when he was fined for handling a stolen motor. A spell dabbling in second-hand cars soon followed. Then, in 1976, he moved into a highly lucrative coin-dealing venture based in posh Mount Street, Mayfair. A switch into the furniture business led to a serious clash with the law at Bristol Crown Court in 1980 when he received two suspended six-month jail sentences for fraud. Palmer then moved into the jewellery trade in the West Country.

But he first came to the attention of Britain's premier team of thief-takers – the Flying Squad – when he was thought to be helping the Brink's-Mat gang melt down their gold bullion. Many police and villains alleged that Palmer kept some of the gold for himself and used the cash proceeds to go into the timeshare business in southern Spain.

When Spanish authorities got to hear about his alleged involvement in handling the proceeds of Brink's-Mat and a number of other high-profile crimes, he was invited to leave Spain, so he did a moonlight flit to Rio de Janeiro. Palmer then went and surprised his criminal associates and the police by volunteering to return to Britain to face trial for handling the Brink's-Mat gold. 'He was supremely confident that he would be acquitted,' recalls one old criminal associate. 'Some of us reckoned he had some kind of "arrangement" with someone. But no one had ever been able to really put the finger on him.'

In 1987, Palmer found himself at the Old Bailey charged with conspiring with Kenneth Noye and his associate Brian Reader to dishonestly handle that Brink's-Mat gold. So many villains were lining up to take a pop at Palmer by this time that he wore body armour throughout the trial.

But Palmer's supreme self-confidence proved entirely justified when, after all the evidence was heard, the jury believed he was innocent and he walked free from the court. Typically, Palmer couldn't resist blowing a contemptuous kiss to detectives.

John Palmer insisted from that moment on that the police began a vendetta against him. His claims sounded mighty familiar to those of his old mate Noye, who often said the cops were out to get him. Rumours that Palmer was an informant who'd swapped certain information with detectives to keep them off his back were fiercely denied by all and sundry.

'They have done anything to try and get me, and have spent millions and millions of pounds of public money to get me. I am not guilty,' he yelled after the Brink's-Mat trial.

Palmer then quickly set up a string of thirteen timeshare resorts in Tenerife, in the Canary Islands, where tens of thousands of tourists would eventually be swindled out of their savings. Vast numbers of innocent punters were systematically tricked into buying timeshare apartments in Tenerife. They handed over large sums of money, which in many cases turned out to be their life savings after falling victim to lies and false promises made to them in a slick, well-orchestrated and thoroughly dishonest sales operation. They included retired police officers, war heroes and even a former trading standards officer.

In 1991, John Palmer turned up in court yet again; this time he copped an 18-month jail sentence – suspended for two years – after admitting an £85,000 swindle using false names to obtain mortgages.

Meanwhile, Palmer continued expanding his timeshare resort and his companies targeted existing timeshare owners through a rent/sell racket, or sold holidaymakers timeshares with the promise of the vast profits they could earn from letting them. The promise of a definite resell of the properties was the inducement to the punters to buy into Palmer's operation.

His salesmen approached tourists with scratch-cards and told them they had won fantastic prizes, such as watches or trips to Disneyland. They were then asked to pick up the prizes from a luxury resort and when they arrived they were given a guided tour.

Palmer's sales staff then offered to sell tourists' existing timeshare apartments if they bought a new one at the resort ... but the original timeshares were never sold, leaving the victims heavily in debt.

Seduced by the Palmer-approved sales patter, those victims paid a deposit by credit card before being confronted with complicated and deliberately misleading paperwork. They were told their other timeshares would be sold within weeks but were urged to take out a loan to buy one of the new apartments, just in case.

Palmer's salesmen then advised them to contact certain finance companies to get the loan and particular resale companies to handle the sale of their old timeshares. But when their old apartments failed to sell and they tried to cancel their contracts they were unable to recover their money and lost thousands of pounds.

And even if the victims did not have a timeshare to trade, Palmer's army got them to buy one and told them that the rental they would charge over the first few years would pay for the purchase.

The irony of all this is that Palmer believed that by pouring all his ill-gotten gains into a (sort of) legit business like timeshare he would be able to live like a king and avoid the problems associated with his earlier criminal enterprises.

'The problem was that John Palmer couldn't run his business like a normal, honest person,' says one retired detective. 'He couldn't resist going for the maximum con, putting pressure on innocent people. Palmer believed the world was full of mugs and he was going to con the lot of them. And he very nearly got away with it ...'

* * *

John 'Goldfinger' Palmer served just over half his term, but soon found himself in trouble again when was arrested in 2007 on fraud charges. He was released on bail after two years in a Spanish prison.

Fast forward to June 2015 when newly retired John 'Goldfinger' Palmer discovered that gangsters never rest in peace: a lone gunman jumped over the wall of his new, isolated Essex country home and shot him dead.

What goes around, comes around.

Chapter 9

PAUL FERRIS

Paul Ferris is feared and respected on the mean streets of Glasgow; one of the wealthiest gangsters in the city's history. And that's quite an achievement when you consider that this Scottish city has been steeped in crime for more than a century.

Back in 1991, hardman Paul Ferris found himself up on charges of murder, kneecapping and drug dealing. He was accused of rubbing out big-time Glasgow drugs dealer Arthur Thompson outside his home in the city. At the time, Thompson, then 31, was serving an 11-year sentence for heroin dealing and was home on a three-day leave from prison.

The court case later starring Paul Ferris featured testimony from a bunch of Glasgow gangsters, all contradicting themselves about Paul's alleged role as one of Scotland's most notorious faces. Paul, then just 28, smiled broadly as the jury read out their 'not guilty' verdict. It was almost as if he knew he'd walk out of there a free man.

No doubt the jury noticed his 'chib', a scar from a knife slash, which runs from the right side of his mouth and curves down below his jawline. The Ferris hearing had been the longest murder trial in Scottish history, costing almost £1 million. Paul and his family come from Blackhill, a council estate in the north east of Glasgow. Everyone on the manor knew the Ferrises and the Thompsons had been waging a deadly turf war for years before Paul ended up in the dock.

Paul Ferris started in the game at a very young age. Bullied as a kid at school in the Glasgow tenements, by the time he was thirteen he'd been sucked into a life of violence in order to escape that childhood aggro. Paul later admitted that hitting back was the best way he could gain respect from his fellow teenagers. 'It also helped me protect myself from serious harm.'

Ferris always carried a weapon. As he said, casually, with a shrug of the shoulders, 'I've always used a weapon of sorts – whether it be a baseball bat or knife.' Yet it could have all been so different for Paul. He'd been virtually adopted by Arthur Thompson Snr, who befriended the then teenager after he copped a firearms conviction before turning sixteen. Old man Thompson took Paul on as a debt collector, or 'enforcer' as they're known in the trade.

Thompson Snr has never said what he thinks about the fact Paul Ferris was the prime suspect in the later contract killing of his son. But from the moment he was cleared of the Thompson charges Paul Ferris was closely monitored by the police who were convinced a hitman would one day execute him.

Paul's gained a lot of respect down the years by always refusing to cough up to the full extent of his involvement in organised crime in Glasgow. But he did once admit, 'That doesn't mean you've to let people stand on your toes. For if they do that, you have got to jump on their neck and break it.' But Paul sticks to brief public statements that guarantee the legend of Paul Ferris continues to grow. It's crystal clear that Paul Ferris's violent habits – he had a tendency to get involved in aggro at the drop of a hat – coupled with his level head, quick mind and easy charm made him one of the most influential gangsters of the Nineties.

But Paul has played it all down. He doesn't even look much like a hardman. He's not physically intimidating. He looks more like a tame businessman in his suit with his mobile phone ringing constantly. He smiles a lot and talks with a quiet tone that hardly ever goes beyond a whisper. 'But you cross him at your peril,' says one who should know.

Just ask the cops in Manchester. He was acquitted of possessing crack cocaine in Lancashire after convincing a jury in the city that he was taking the highly addictive drug to improve his skin. 'How he got away with that I'll never know,' says one thief taker bitterly.

Not surprisingly, Paul is constantly looking over his shoulder. When he was pulled up on the M4 one time after being chased at 130mph by cops in an unmarked Merc he claimed he thought it was full of hitmen. 'There have been events in the past where guns have been fired from strange vehicles,' he later explained. Once again no charges were preferred against the renowned gangster.

Many in Glasgow believe that Paul Ferris's fury with the Thompson family was sparked by the violence inflicted on his own father Willie Ferris. In the 18 months before Paul went for trial on those charges of murdering Arthur Thompson Jnr, Paul's dad was beaten about the head with a hammer and baseball bat, knocked to the ground and slashed with a razor. After one attack he needed 100 stitches.

Meanwhile, Paul's elder brother, Billy, a convicted murderer who was given permission to move to a jail closer to his disabled father, continues to insist, 'I'm the only killer in the Ferris family.'

And throughout all this, Paul Ferris was alleged to be involved in a drugs operation which was netting at least £20,000 a week supplying virtually all the heroin in Glasgow – a city of 900,000 where there are 12,500 injecting drug addicts.

In the Nineties, as the legend of Paul Ferris grew and grew, so did the number of his encounters with local law enforcement. Inevitably, the man other villains jealously call 'Houdini' eventually found himself boxed into a corner.

Paul landed in hot water after a bizarre incident hundreds of miles from Glasgow when police in Lancashire boarded a night train on which a rowdy Scotsman was drinking heavily and annoying other passengers. He turned out to be armed with a .22 pistol, a silencer and 60 rounds – standard kit for a hitman.

The next day, while this would-be shootist was being held by the Old Bill, a number of frantic calls were received on his mobile phone and pager. Those calls linked him to Paul Ferris and a bunch of other Glasgow hoods. The cops then put the thumbscrews on their drunken hitman. They knew this was a chance to nick Houdini – Paul Ferris.

Undercover police mounted an operation to shadow Paul and his suspected arms dealing ring. They watched as Paul helped load three machine guns, silencers, four detonators and a box of ammo into a car after paying out £4,700 to a gun dealer right slap bang in the middle of the Adams Family's manor in Islington, North London. Amongst the weapons were special blue-tipped bullets which travel below the speed of sound so there's less of a bang when they're fired. The cops rapidly concluded Paul was a member of an arms gang on a run from Glasgow to London. They moved in and nicked the lot of them.

Paul and three others eventually found themselves at the Old Bailey where they all denied conspiracy to sell or transfer prohibited weapons and conspiracy to deal in firearms with three others. They also denied possession of explosives. Paul defended himself in court by claiming he thought the box in which the weapons were found contained material for a fraud he was involved in. He told the court he had no idea there were weapons in the box. The court heard how Paul Ferris was spotted putting all the armoury in a green Nissan Prairie, destination unknown. The Old Bill even found the £4,700 in Scottish banknotes in a jiffy bag that had Paul's fingerprints on it.

Paul, who at the time gave his address as Hogganfield Street, Glasgow, was eventually jailed for ten years for his part in the gun-running operation. It turned out all the weapons were on their way to gangs of villains in Manchester, Liverpool and Glasgow, for whom Ferris had become the main supplier. Judge Henry Blacksell told Paul Ferris after convicting him, 'One hardly dares speculate the potential death and destruction that may have been caused if they had reached their intended destination.'

Serving his sentence for gun-running, Paul found himself locked up and bored in Frankland Jail,

Durham, so he decided to pen his life story in a book. Paul, who freely admitted delivering some serious stabbings to rivals and beating up others, insisted in the book he was harrassed and framed by the police and two of Scotland's most powerful gangsters.

Like so many of the other faces featured in this book, this is by no means the last we will hear of Paul Ferris, who was released from prison in 1999.

* * *

Paul Ferris decided to 'go straight' after his release from prison and now works as a business consultant, but admitted to the *Scottish Sun* in 2018 that he still keeps an eye on the goings-on in Glasgow.

Chapter 10

THE HOLLOW HIPPY

The boys in blue reckon drugs baron Andrew Billimore has made a whopping £600 million as a premier league dealer over the past 20 years. Even if he's only made a tenth of that he's worth a place in this book. Andy's network is so vast that at one point the Old Bill claimed he was boasting of importing coke worth up to £2 million a week.

Yet the 35-year-old former Cathedral guide (I kid thee not) has officially been 'unemployed' throughout this period. But then Andy Billimore is a master at keeping things low key. No flash motors, luxury mansions or fancy women for Andy.

He's studiously avoided the champagne-popping, coke-sniffing lifestyle that all his drugs have no doubt sparked in others. His semi-detached home in a row of former council houses is run-down with a rusting old caravan sitting on the pavement outside. So where the hell is all his dosh?

The police remain convinced he's got it stashed away in a secret burial site or dotted around the world in foreign bank accounts. His girlfriend insisted he was broke after Andy's empire was exposed to the world when he was nicked in June 1999. But she would, wouldn't she?

Andy was caught in possession of 104kg of puff in his van which he'd just shipped in from Holland. It later turned out that one of his mates had grassed him up to the Old Bill. Detectives were told about a wooded area where more drugs were found plus £23,500 cash in his very tatty home. But there was no sign of the tens of millions of quid.

The beginning of the end for Andy came when his half-brother Tom McTaggart was nicked at Heathrow with £69,700 in cash, later found to be covered in traces of amphetamine and other drugs. A list of 'clients' was then found in McTaggart's house. He and Andy Billimore eventually came up with a great excuse; they reckoned the list was part of a Monopoly-style game called Skin-Up which they were devising together!

But even the cops said they were baffled by Andy's modest life in his £65,000 former council house in the village of Little Downham, Cambridgeshire. They produced evidence he was buying mountains of Charlie from Holland for £20,000 per kilogram and he'd even linked up with the Colombians for £16,000 per kilo. One of Andy's mates said he boasted he was importing 50 kilograms every three days.

One policeman explained, 'Drugs baron is the right word for him. He's a top league dealer. He'd had a few previous convictions. But successful drugs dealers don't get caught very.often. That's why they're successful.'

In September 2000, Andy was sent down for 20 years when he admitted conspiracy to supply puff, supplying puff and plotting to pervert the course of justice. He was also found guilty of conspiring to supply Charlie. His half-brother, former paratrooper Tom McTaggart, also copped a long stretch following their two-week trial at Norwich Crown Court.

Andy was ordered to pay more than half a million quid within 12 months or face an extra four years on his sentence. As he sat in the dock, cuffed and surrounded by armed police, he shook his head when the fine was mentioned. Then Andy looked over to his live-in partner, sitting in the public gallery and motioned a telephone sign with his thumb and little finger. At the time of writing Andy still hasn't paid up the money. Naturally, his close friends and family insist he doesn't have the money. Andy claims to this day he was 'fitted up'.

The police think otherwise. 'He's one of the cleverest drug suppliers we've ever come across. He thought he'd never get nicked because he hid all his fortune so carefully, but we know he's one of the richest villains in Britain.'

Chapter 11

HITMAN JAKE

There's no shortage of work for a good hitman in today's Britain. The number of shootists on our streets has reached epidemic proportions. Twenty years ago, if you wanted someone bumped off there was only a small crew of highly professional killers-for-hire available. But in the year 2000, there were at least fifty rub-outs in Britain – and those are the ones the police know about.

Mind you, professional hits get little newspaper coverage. As old Fleet Street crime hack Peter Wilson says, 'One villain knocking off another doesn't have the same news appeal as a beautiful brunette blasting her cheating hubby to death.'

Hitmen themselves revel in the low-key nature of their business. Says one, 'The less publicity the better. The papers don't seem that interested in most hits.' Even the cozzers play down such crimes. As one detective explains, 'We take the attitude that every time there's a hit it means one less villain on the streets – and that can't be a bad thing.'

But now even the Met's finest admit the situation has grown completely out of control. They've set up a special squad to crack down on these so-called criminal renegades. David Veness, Assistant Commissioner in charge of specialist operations, admits, 'We have a genuine fear that there is a greater capacity for criminals to gain access to individuals willing to kill for money. There is clear evidence that there are small groups for whom this is the main form of criminal activity.' That's copspeak for: 'It's a big problem.'

The bottom line is that life's a lot cheaper in the twenty-first century than it was when sawn-off-shotgun-toting armed robbers swaggered across pavements taking pot shots at the Sweeney, as the plain clothes boys crouched behind their Ford Granadas. These days small-time hoods are prepared to knock off other villains, cheating lovers and work rivals. Some of the real pros are in danger of being put out of business.

Take my man Jake. He's been in 'the business' for twelve years, lives in a nice, comfortable three-bed bungalow in the Kent countryside, and no one other than his dear old mum, and his wife and kids knows his real identity. That's the way he intends to keep it. 'The fellows who hire me don't give a toss who I am. But I've got their respect. I do the job clean and simple with no fuckin' aggro,' explains Jake.

Jake reckons the hired hand who popped million-aire-gangster-turned-police-informant Pete McNeil, alias James Lawton, on 10 February 1998 didn't put a foot wrong. Coke-and-hooker addict McNeil, 40, was iced at point-blank range outside his very respectable, commuter-belt, redbrick modern detached home on the Bow Field housing estate in the twee Hampshire village of Hook. 'That was a classic hit,' says Jake. 'McNeil had it comin' for years.'

The victim had even been proudly telling people there was 'a bullet out there with my name on it' from the moment he turned supergrass when he was nicked for involvement in a $70 million coke heist. The drugs ring had links with an American branch of the Mafia in Detroit, not to mention a number of Medellin men from Colombia. So when McNeil finally got the bullet on his own doorstep at 8.01pm as a pot of pasta simmered on the stove, there wasn't a lot of grieving.

The list of suspects was longer than Michael Jordan's arm. There were criminal associates he'd double-crossed, ripped-off call girls, pissed-off coke dealers and even some poor mug who bought a second-hand car off McNeil and discovered it was a hot motor.

While no one can deny that Pete McNeil had it coming, there is no excuse for murder when hitmen shoot innocent people. That's what happened when little Dillon Hull, still clutching a toy, was hit twice in the head after a hired killer shot his 28-year-old stepdad John Bates in the stomach. Bates was a small-time smackhead/pusher on the lam from some big-time dope dealers in the unlikely setting of Bolton, Lancs. He was a recognised soldier in a vicious local drugs war while five-year-old Dillon was the innocent kid literally caught in the crossfire. Even hardened hitmen like my man Jake were gutted by the killing. 'It's fuckin' outrageous. Takin' a kid out like that. Makes me sick to think 'bout it.'

Within hours of the Dillon shooting, on 7 August 1997, the police were flooded with calls from local villains offering their services to help find the pratt who carried out probably the most cowardly hit ever witnessed on mainland Britain. 'There are too many fuckin' loose canons carryin' out hits in exchange for a fix or a second-hand Fiesta. It's out of control ... and it's gonna get worse,' says one retired drug dealer from south east London.

Back in June and July 1998, a posse of London Yardies commissioned three barbaric murders, including the hitman-style execution of two young mothers. The Met linked the slayings after forensic tests revealed the victims were shot with the same 9mm self-loading shooter. The posse plugged mums Avril Johnson and Michelle Carby by shooting them in the head at their own homes. The bodies were discovered by their own kids.

The same Yardie firm rubbed out 34-year-old Patrick Ferguson, inside his own home in Kingsbury, North London. Each of the victims was linked to drug supply networks that ran right across London from Brixton to Stratford, where each of the women lived. The shootists were utterly ruthless; they terrorised and sexually assaulted their victims in a deliberate attempt to send a deadly message to their drug-dealing rivals.

'This sorta thing might happen in Kingston, Jamaica, or Cali, Colombia, even the east side of LA, but not London, for fuck's sake,' says one old-time villain. 'It's completely out of order.'

Gun violence spawned by the Yardie posses has escalated dramatically in recent years. Of 160 murders in London in 1997, 41 victims were black and 18 of those were shot in classic Yardie-style hits. To put this into prospective the black population of London only comprises 8% of the entire city.

Crack-smoking, Uzi-toting Yardies make the shootist who iced 57-year-old Great Train Robber Charlie Wilson by the pool of his 250 grand Marbella hacienda look like pussycats. 'It was a classic hit except that Wilson was a known face and that meant the police here and in Spain worked doubly hard to try and solve the case,' says one insider.

Wilson's killer was a pro called Billy Edmonds, 35. He rubbed Charlie out before freewheeling off, bizarrely, on a mountain bike. Not far down the hill he jumped into a motor driven by Danny 'Scarface' Roff – whose nickname came from the distinctive scar under his right eye and who had a fondness for chunky gold jewellery. At the time Scarface was on the run after escaping with Edmonds from a British nick while serving 13 years for armed robbery. Edmonds has been on the lam ever since.

Cops I know assure me that Wilson's murder, in April 1990, was commissioned on the orders of Londoner Roy Atkins, who had been told Wilson had crossed him by allowing an arrested drug dealer to name him as a drug gang leader in return for a lighter sentence. Sounds like a case of dog eat dog. Atkins got his comeuppance when he took three bullets to the head while negotiating an E deal in an Amsterdam nighterie. Public enemy Roff was re-arrested shortly afterwards as an escaped convict. But the Guardia Civil could never pin the Wilson job on him and the Dutch failed to nab him for the killing of Atkins, either.

So Roff was soon out of clink. In 1993 he took part in rubbing out another rival villain, property tycoon Donald Urquart. Urquart, 55, was shot three times in front of his girlfriend in Marylebone High Street, in central London. As one of Charlie Wilson's mates once told me, 'Trouble is, these things are never final. Each killing sparks more shootings which means a lot more faces will keep hitting the deck.'

Triggerman Scarface has since been linked to at least half a dozen other professional rub-outs. So it was hardly a surprise when he took his last breath on the driveway of his comfortable, mock-tudor detached mansion in Bromley, Kent, in March 1997. Already partly disabled from another failed attempt on his life, Scarface struggled out of his Mercedes 500SL into a wheelchair. At that moment the double doors of a rusting white Escort van parked a few yards away swung open and two fellows in black balaclavas and hoods opened fire. They hit Roff in the head and chest before burning rubber as the van's doors flapped while they careered away from the scene of the crime. They dumped the van half a mile down the road.

Life comes even cheaper if you mix it with the Triads. When they hit rival gang members it usually goes unreported – and unsolved – because of their Mafia-style secrecy and the fears of victims and witnesses. The four main societies – the 14K, We On Lok, Wo Shing Wo and San Yee On – rake in vast profits from protection rackets on restaurants and businesses, prostitution, fraud, illegal immigration and illicit gambling. That means there's plenty of work for their handpicked shootists.

One hit-man called Wai Hen Cheung, known as George in Soho, was even specially initiated into the Triads. George had to have his blood pricked from a finger into a glass of wine. Then he was instructed to join a gun club in Chingford, Essex, to learn how to handle lethal weapons. He was also given a job in a Chinese takeaway on the Channel Island of Guernsey so that his face would not be known around Soho while he was training up for his first hit. George later shot Hong Kong businessman Ying Kit Lam, 31, in a contract job intended to punish Lam and deter others from crossing the deadly Triads. But Lam lived, although he was crippled for life. George was sent down last year for a very long time.

Final word has to go to my man Jake, renowned as one of the most feared shootists on the streets of south east England. 'The rules of the game are changin' every day. My basic price is 20 grand, unless I'm bein' asked to take out a big-time face who's got a lot of protection. I always get paid in full, in advance, in cash. How else could I handle it, take a cheque? There are other unwritten clauses that go into every hit contract. If I get nicked the geezer commissioning the hit takes care of all my legal costs plus my bail if I manage to get it. He'd also make sure I was comfortable in the nick, that my missus was comfortable at home, as well as do everything to try and get me out. Finally, when

I finished my bird, he would have a bundle of cash waiting for me. This is done to guarantee silence. As long as all obligations are taken care of, I'm not going to say a word to no one. I'm certainly not going to land anyone in the shit. They'd soon finish me off.'

But Jake says it's not the risk of being caught for his crimes that bothers him. 'There are other so-called pros out there poppin' people for five grand a piece. But you get what you pay for and these cut-price operators all get caught in the end and then they start singing. Let's face it, a granny in Blackpool who wants shot of her old man after thirty years of abuse is goin' to end up hiring a fuckin' amateur or an undercover cozzer.

'There's too many wideboys makin' out they can carry out hits for two and six. All they do is make problems for blokes like me.' But Jake reckons he has the answer. 'I'm plannin' to retire soon. Buy myself a nice little villa on the Costa Del Sol and start relaxin' and enjoyin' my life.' He pauses and nods his head slowly. 'If I live that long ...'

Chapter 12

FRANK THE SMUGGLER

Frank is the head of a gang of smugglers who have been renowned in the British underworld for more than forty years. Now aged 74, Frank first began in this line of work in the early 1970s when he organised lorry-loads of hash to the UK from India and Afghanistan. Frank's transport company is still running to this day as a legitimate business, which on the surface deals mostly in fruit imported from the Far East.

Throughout his youth in south east London and Kent in the late 1950s and 1960s, Frank was a member of a gang of professional bank robbers. He even worked at one time with members of the Great Train Robbery gang just before they pulled off the so-called Crime of the Century in 1963. Frank was a renowned 'transport man' – the guy who waited in the getaway car to drive the robbers at high speed away from the scene of their crimes.

'Those were good times back then,' explained Frank. 'Robbers like us were treated like pop stars and we had the lot – wine, women and song. But I knew it was a risky business, so I kept my eyes and ears open for something else, something more secure.

'I knew nothing about drugs back then. In fact, they were the devil's candy as far as me and most of my mates were concerned. No one touched an aspirin let alone a line of cocaine back in those days. We used to sneer at people who smoked pot and label them 'stupid hippies' and stuff like that.'

But Frank says the turning point in his attitude towards drugs came when he served a short stretch in prison in the late 1960s. 'That's when I first came across the stuff. I smoked a bit in jail to help pass the time away but I never really got into it like a lot of other people inside. I always preferred a pint or a vodka tonic and still do to this day.

'But seeing what was happening in prison convinced me that drugs were about to explode onto the streets and soon everyone would want them. I was an opportunist and I wanted a piece of that action. So not long after I got out of prison I put together a proposition to another villain I knew and we arranged to buy a big load of hash from Lebanon, which was infamous for its Lebanese Gold back then.

'The only problem was we had to get the stuff back from the Middle East. We'd paid rock bottom prices for the actual drugs but we were going to be ripped off by a bunch of dodgy smugglers, who'd end up taking most of our profit in 'transport fees' and probably nick half the hash as well for good measure.

'So I looked into what sort of legitimate goods usually got exported from Lebanon and oranges looked the perfect cover. Well, that clinched it. I decided I'd send a lorry over to pick up some oranges and we'd hide the hash under them.'

Frank then launched a legitimate transport company, which he officially registered then painted the name of the firm on the side of the truck that was going to pick up the hash.

'That first collection was certainly an interesting experience. Me and a mate headed off to Lebanon by road. It was a hairy old drive through some quite dodgy countries but we never had a sniff of trouble. We picked up the oranges and then the hash in Beirut and drove back. We eventually got through customs in Dover without any problems. I knew then and there this was going to be my long-term criminal career.'

But back then, many of Frank's fellow gangsters still disapproved of drug smuggling, so he was very careful not to let them know what he and his gang were up to.

'I genuinely feared one of them might grass me up to the law because they would have thought I was scum of the earth to smuggle drugs, even puff as we called hash back then.

'So it was a risky move. But the profit I was soon making made it more than worth it for me. I was hooked. I'd struck gold and back then the chances of being caught smuggling were virtually nil.'

Within five years, Frank's transport company had grown to a dozen lorries and he was even making a healthy profit from the 'honest' exportation of fruit and vegetables, on top of his vast rake-offs from hash smuggling.

'It's funny cos none of my mates really cottoned on to what I was up to. They all just thought my legit transport business had hit the jackpot and that's the way I liked to keep it.'

But Frank feared that one of the big London criminal families at that time might try and muscle in on his business. 'I knew there were people circling my company and trying to work out how I was doing so well. But I kept on smiling and making out the fruit and veg business was booming, and most of them fell for it.'

Ironically, it was actually one of Britain's last truly big heists that made things much more complicated for Frank's business. 'In 1983, some of my old South London mates were involved in the Brink's-Mat robbery. It was the biggest bullion raid of all time and the police went AWOL trying to round up any known associates of the gang. I was one of their prime targets just because I'd been involved in some blaggings in the years before I set up my transport business.'

'The cozzers presumed my transport company had been used to take some of the gold bullion abroad. They raided my company just as a lorry returned from a run to Turkey. The police found a massive stash of hash, I got nicked and had to close the whole operation down. I got five years for that little caper.'

Frank insists to this day he was innocent of handling any of the Brink's-Mat gold bullion. He explained: 'The coppers were after me for anything. They knew I'd been in the smuggling game for years and they were going to get me for something. I had to accept my sentence as part of my job. Simple as that.'

When Frank emerged from prison a few years later, he set up another transport company. But this time he was even more careful than before. 'I ran it entirely as a 100% legitimate business importing and exporting fruit and veg. I did that for more than a year after I got out of prison. It drove the coppers mad because they raided my premises three times during that period, convinced I was up to no good. But I knew I had to keep my nose clean for a while.'

Frank's dislike of the police was, he says, fuelled by the attitude of the London police back then. He explains: 'In those days, the cozzers harrassed me non-stop. They'd sit by the gates to my house in cars and generally make a right pest of themselves. They enjoyed putting me through the wringer but I knew that when the time was right I'd set up another smuggling operation and they wouldn't even get a sniff of it.'

By 1990, Frank's police 'shadows' had pulled away after failing to arrest him for any more offences. 'That was the perfect moment to get back into the hash game. Within less than a year my gang was running as many shipments as before I'd been sent down. It was magic.'

Frank looks on himself as the ultimate survivor. 'Look, most of my old mates from South London are either dead or in prison. They sneered at me for getting involved in the hash game all those years ago. Then a lot of them finally woke up to the money that could be made from drugs but went into the coke business, which seemed to be an easier option because it's less bulky than hash and easier to hide. But coke's a completely different ballgame. The stakes are higher and so are the risks, which is why so many of them either got shot or ended up being nicked for long sentences.'

Frank eventually began slowing down and he sold off the main part of his transport business to another criminal, who subsequently got arrested and jailed for drug smuggling. 'It didn't surprise me. This bloke didn't have a clue how to run a successful smuggling operation. He got blown out of the water when one of his drivers decided to grass him up. It would never have happened if I'd still been running the firm.'

These days, Frank runs a 'small smuggling operation', which uses just two lorries. He admits that sometimes he has smuggled refugees across the English Channel. 'It's a different ballgame from hash. Some of my closest mates would be appalled if they knew I was dipping my toe into people smuggling but it's the best money you can make these days.'

Frank is reluctant to talk about the specifics of his most recent people smuggling operation, except to say: 'I did it a few times and I'm not proud of it. Those poor bastards are so desperate to get here that a lot of villains are taking money from them but often not providing the transport they promise. I've delivered all the people I took money from but now I recognise that there are too many cowboys running people smuggling operations across the Channel, so I've pulled out of doing any more runs.'

Frank added: 'Maybe it is finally time to quit while I'm ahead.'

Chapter 13

THE
SPECIALISTS

THE FIXER

Immigration officer Guy Emmett has earned his place in this gangster hall of fame because without the 'fixers' of this world there would be no underworld. He's made a fortune from bribes by allowing illegal immigrants to stay in Britain as well as 'nodding through' a number of 'iffy'-looking passports being used by some of the most notorious faces on our streets today. As a pass-port officer at Gatwick Airport, Emmett was supposed to stop people illegally entering the country. Instead he started letting them in at a cost of up to £4,000 a time.

The scam enabled Emmett, on a modest salary of £20,000 a year, to live a millionaire's lifestyle. He splashed out on a £50,000 Porsche Carrera, a TVR sportscar, a BMW and a Lotus Elise. He bagged a total of seven properties, some of which were paid for with cash. In one eight-month period his bank accounts showed that Emmett was spending cash at a rate of £1,000 a day. While immigrants were his bread and butter, it was the fat cat criminals who made up his *crème de la crème*.

When Emmett was finally brought to justice, Home Office investigators only managed to trace 76 people allowed into the country illegally by Emmett. But they believed the true figure could be approaching 1,000.

Guy Emmett's criminal career took off shortly after he was posted to Gatwick's South Terminal in 1992 and continued for almost five years. Emmett ran the scam with 41-year-old immigration lawyer and adviser Christian Jideofo, himself an illegal immigrant from Nigeria who'd undergone a marriage of convenience in order to stay in Britain.

Soon Emmett was not only providing people with entry into this country but was also stamping passports so they were given indefinite leave to remain and travel abroad, meaning they could come and go from Britain without any restrictions. He was a dream 'fixer' for many underworld figures who preferred to travel in and out of Britain on dodgy passports than allow the authorities to keep an eye on their movements.

As prosecutor Mark Gadsen explained at Emmett's Old Bailey trial, 'He systematically endorsed passports of foreigners who had no right to remain here with stamps that would be accepted by the authorities and give them the right to stay here.'

Emmett used his own official stamp and that of a colleague to endorse the passports. In 1993 he even set up his own immigration advisory business, called

Stephen Goodfellows, in Thornton Heath, Surrey, even though that was strictly against the terms of his employment. Soon word got out that he was an immigration officer with few scruples if the price was right.

His mate, Jideofo, who operated from offices in Kilburn, north west London, sent his 'clients' to Emmett. Jideofo also sent passports to Emmett, who would enter official stamps. Clients paid deposits of up to £2,000 beforehand plus the balance on receipt of the stamped passports.

Those official stamps also smoothed the path to British citizenship for at least 50% of his 'customers' by indicating the passport holders had been checked out and deemed suitable for residency. Jideofo also arranged for bogus letters purporting to show the holders had been allowed UK residency.

'Clients' were even provided with a crib sheet of what to say if they were challenged at a port of entry. Their details had all been entered on the Home Office computer and they were told to tell any suspicious official, 'Check my passport with the computer.' Their written instructions finished by stating, 'Don't panic, don't change your story and everything will be all right.'

Guy Emmett's reign as the passport king of Gatwick only came to an end when a suspicious solicitor contacted the chief immigration officer. Emmett was arrested the following year, in June 1996, but not charged until 1999. He steadfastly insisted that although the stamps in the passports were bogus he was not the culprit.

Emmett, of Furze Lane, Purley, Surrey, and Jideofo, of Kingston Road, New Barnet, Hertfordshire, were convicted of conspiring to defraud the Home Secretary and assist illegal immigrants to enter the UK. Emmett's wife Elizabeth, 30, also an immigration officer at Gatwick, was cleared of any involvement on the direction of the judge halfway through the six-week trial. A third man, Sam Essuah, who gave evidence for the prosecution, had earlier been jailed for 12 months in 1998 after admitting four immigration offences. He introduced many paying customers to Emmett.

Guy Emmett was eventually sentenced to eight years in prison. Judge Timothy Pontius told the 35-year-old villain that his greed had led him 'without regret or shame to betray the high standards of integrity and trust' expected of immigration officials. His partner Jideofo got a six-and-a-half-year stretch.

But it wasn't all bad new for fixer Guy Emmett. The police reckon he's got a small fortune stashed away in the Channel Isles. And no doubt he'll be dabbling in some stocks and shares while he's watching the daisies grow from his cell window.

THE SUPERGRASS

No book about gangsters in the twenty-first century would be complete without a look inside the world of the 'supergrass'. Without informants, it's highly unlikely that any gangsters would ever be apprehended.

Computer nerd Martin Grant was recruited from inside Blantyre House open prison in Kent to help a bunch of notorious gangsters, including Kenny Noye and John 'Little Legs' Lloyd, set up a credit card scam they believed could net them tens of millions of pounds. Grant – jailed for attempting to murder his wife and child – had studied for a degree in electronic communications while in the slammer.

Eventually, he was allowed out of prison on a day-release programme for work experience at a van hire business owned by Paul Kidd, another villain involved with Noye and Lloyd's cashcard cloning scheme. The gang planned to enter British Telecom exchanges with a team of corrupt engineers to put telephone taps on the lines and memory boards. This information was then to be transferred to the gang's computer.

In mid-summer of 1995, the gang enjoyed a champagne dinner at a Kent hotel. Six prostitutes were then hired for £3,000 for the entire night to service all the crooks. Amongst the villains was nerdy computer wizard Martin Grant. Unknown to the gang, Grant – who was plainly out of his depth amongst this team of veritable hardmen – was already feeding information about the credit card scam to police. He'd earlier confessed to a prison chaplain about the planned robbery before making a statement of over 300 pages to Scotland Yard detectives.

Grant got cold feet that evening because he didn't want to sleep with any hookers, let alone the ones specially recruited in London's West End by Kenny Noye. Noye was infuriated and only agreed to keep Grant on the team because his computer knowledge was invaluable.

Grant was doubly nervous because he knew he was a dead man if any of the gang found out he was double-crossing them. Eventually, he forced himself to sleep with one girl in case it gave him away. It was a disaster and the other gang members made fun of him because of his failure to perform.

* * *

On 25 July 1995, police raided a farmhouse in Yalding, Kent, and seized more than 70,000 blank cashcards plus 28 computer disks. A murder contract was immediately put out on computer boffin-turned-supergrass Martin Grant. Noye and the rest of the gang knew he'd stitched them up. 'The word went out that certain faces were prepared to pay double the going rate

[£20,000] to get Grant plugged,' one retired villain later recalled.

As Roy Ramm, one of the senior detectives involved in the case, later explained, 'The scam was a classic example of a group of South London robbers and villains who saw an opportunity to get a great deal of money, but did not have the technical expertise so they worked outside their circle and brought in somebody [Grant] who eventually destroyed them.'

Some years later, Martin Grant came out of hiding to reveal what it felt like to double-cross so-called master criminals Kenny Noye and John 'Little Legs' Lloyd. 'They were just names to me at first. They meant nothing. But people inside Blantyre House talked about them as if they were gods,' he recalled.

Grant insists he tried to walk away from the scam. 'I said I thought it wouldn't work. But another inmate told me if I wasn't careful I'd lose my eye. That's when I contacted the police.'

Grant said he attended one meeting with the gang where Noye produced prison paperwork on his (Grant's) record and family background which clearly had been given to Noye by prison staff. Those details included the addresses of Grant's mother and brother.

Then, in a chilling incident, John 'Little Legs' Lloyd drove Grant up to his mother's house and walked him through the front door, even introducing himself to

Grant's mother, 'just to let me know he knew where she lived'. Grant added, 'John Lloyd then phoned Kenny Noye to say he had met my mum. I was so scared.' Grant says that when he decided to go to the police about the scam he was too terrified to report anything to staff at Blantyre House'.

Grant says that Noye became very threatening towards him once he and Lloyd began suspecting he might have grassed on them. 'One time they got a bunch of other villains to follow me back to prison to make sure I wasn't in touch with the police,' he said.

Grant claimed that while still in Blantyre House he was handed £50,000 by an inmate who was given it by a visitor who was a contact of Kenny Noye's. The cash was supposed to secure Grant's role in the scam, but instead he claims he threw it away in disgust. 'I didn't want the money but it shows just how powerful Kenny Noye was that he could get that money to me inside jail,' said Grant.

Then Noye even opened a building society account in Grant's name and started dropping small amounts of cash into it. The gangsters were trying to lock Grant in so he could not back out of the scam or dare to grass them up. They knew he was the weakest link.

Hours before the arrest of the Hole-in-the-Wall suspects including Lloyd (Noye was never charged in connection with the crime even though he was later named in open court), Martin Grant was placed in police custody 'for his own protection'. Detectives put him in a safe house with armed officers 24 hours a day and only moved him by helicopter.

Grant concluded, 'I know they hold a grudge against me and I'm very nervous about it. Remember, I have seen the other side of Kenny Noye, not so much against me but against others who have mucked him about. Although he can be a very nice chap he is quite capable of turning into an aggressor.'

Grant had absolutely no idea what he was letting himself in for when he signed up for the witness protection programme. There are two distinct catagories of protected witnesses. The first is the innocent bystander. If they agree they are given every privilege imaginable and helped to set up a new life. The second category are professional criminals like Martin Grant who turn grass because it is their only choice if they want to avoid more prison sentences.

And the police never let people like Grant forget they are criminals. Rather than being kept in a hotel or safe house, they spend their time being moved between special secure units and police stations. As Grant later said, 'It was worse than the open prison I was already in.'

At the time of writing, Martin Grant was still in hiding, afraid that Kenny Noye and his associates wish to do him harm. His only clue about where he resided was to say, 'It's somewhere north of Watford ...'

THE GUNSMITH

Gangsters are involved in so many heavyweight scenes these days that most of them are tooled up at all times. That means there is a small, select band of armourers – better known as gunsmiths – on duty 24 hours a day.

Ex-Met police officer Sidney Wink was gunsmith numero uno, at the top of his tree. He had the respect and ear of many of London's most fearsome gangsters despite having once been Old Bill. 'But then he had to have some bottle with that background, didn't he?' one old face recently remarked.

Wink's speciality, although never proved in a court of law, was renumbering illegal weapons, including those used by members of the Brink's-Mat gang. (It never ceases to amaze how much of this book connects to Brink's-Mat.)

Sid Wink was also strongly suspected of supplying the guns used in two murders – the 1992 contract killing of Kenny Noye's London money launderer Donald Urquart, and the shooting of PC Patrick Dunne by three Yardie gunmen.

Not surprisingly, Wink's background as a cop made the police even more infuriated by his very existence. As one retired thief taker told me, 'Wink was the pits. A man who had represented law and order only to go across to the other side and even supply a weapon that was used in the shooting of a policeman. He was a bloody disgrace.'

But being a gunsmith is no picnic. Wink found himself dealing with some of the most deadly criminals in Britain, which meant he always had to be on his guard. 'Some of them didn't trust him at first because of his background. You could say Sid overcame more obstacles than most criminals,' says one former police colleague.

By the early Nineties, Sid Wink was starting to feel the pressure that inevitably accompanied such a deadly career move. He was renowned for supplying untraceable weapons, but some villains thought he'd been ripping them off by charging high prices for weapons, so they decided to have a word in the ear of the local constabulary.

'That's when Sid started getting visits from the cozzers at all times of the day and night. He started to get really freaked out and tried to slow down his operation so he was only supplying villains he knew and trusted,' explained one former face.

But in August 1994, a week after officers investigating PC Dunne's murder raided his Essex home, the pressure got too much for old Sid Wink. He put a pistol to his head and pulled the trigger, taking a lot of very tasty secrets with him to his grave.

May the Lord have mercy on his soul ...

Chapter 14

RUSSIAN SUICIDE

TITNESS PARK, SUNNINGHILL,
NEAR ASCOT, BERKSHIRE,
23 MARCH 2014

The naked body lay slumped loosely on the floor up against the ice cold Italian marble bathroom wall.

The face was swollen and cyanosed, the dark staring eyes sightless and fixed, and the white eyeballs haemorrhaging into streaks of scarlet.

Around the angled neck was a constriction: a ligature unusual in that it was made from rope and torn sheets, which had cut deep into the throat. As time passed in the quiet bathroom, the viscid blood – halted in its circulation by the death of the heart – began draining into the lower part of the body.

A thin crack of yellow light showed beneath the closed bathroom door and through the window came the distant murmur of traffic passing the £30 million mansion. As the day progressed, other sounds could be heard: the ticking of a hallway clock, the light tapping of occasional rain showers against the window pane, and the measured footsteps of passing servants.

The bathroom door was eventually forced open by the victim's trusted bodyguard, who entered to find the scene illuminated by a thin strip of warm natural light moving across the pallid corpse.

The bodyguard looked momentarily down at his boss before testing the limp wrist for a pulse, knowing full well he would not find one. Then he moved calmly towards a cupboard next to the body, took out a grey blanket and laid it carefully over the corpse.

Moments later, the same man quietly unlocked the door to a small office on the floor below and entered. Searching deftly and silently he looked through the contents of an open safe and removed papers from it. He next opened and explored with the same attentive care the drawers of a wooden desk followed by steel filing cabinets in the far corner of the room as the gradual fading of the outside light warned of the onset of darkness.

The bodyguard then pulled his mobile out of the inside pocket of his jacket and calmly punched out a number.

Back in the bathroom an hour later, the corpse was lifted by two coroner's officers onto a stretcher containing an open body bag, which was then carefully zipped up. Alongside them, two Scotland Yard police officers in dark suits reminded the medical examiners that a full autopsy would need to be performed.

* * *

This was the latest death by what had become known amongst billionaire money laundering gangsters in London as a 'Russian Suicide', commissioned by one evil gang of billionaire black money mobsters, who have turned London and the south east of England into the most lucrative crime land the world has ever seen.

As one former money launderer called 'Tom' said: 'You didn't fuck with that gang. They liked sending out these sorts of 'messages' to make sure no one was tempted to inform the police about their activities.'

For the past fifteen years, London has been dominated by this one particular gang of billionaire criminals who 'clean' money (i.e. make 'dirty' money made through criminal activity appear to have been legally obtained) for numerous wealthy tycoons prepared to do anything to hold onto their fortunes. These money gangsters project themselves as hard working entrepreneurs and are often protected through their association with senior British politicians, bankers and even members of the Royal Family.

Tom explained: 'You'd never know these guys were gangsters. They were right at the top of London's social scene. Young, immaculately dressed, they often passed themselves off as property developers but we all knew who the actual gang members were because if you tried to steal any business from them, they'd come down on you like a ton of bricks.'

These UK-based money mobsters and their clients – often Russian oligarchs – are even alleged to have paid Russian leader Vladimir Putin and his associates billions of dollars to ensure that Putin didn't target them for the sort of assassination that occurred with the 2018 poisoning of Sergei and Yulia Skripal in Salisbury.

Tom went on: 'These connections with Putin also helped protect the gang from other criminals. Two of the guys at the top of the gang were English, but there were Russians and Eastern Europeans pulling the strings behind them. This was a massive operation.'

And the gang of money launderers themselves used specialist hitmen on at least half a dozen occasions in the UK to silence their enemies. These professional killers often 'dressed up' murders to look like suicides. One alleged victim was Johnny Elichaoff, former husband of British TV star Trinny Woodall.

On 12 November 2014, at Whiteleys shopping centre in Bayswater, Central London, property developer Elichaoff arrived at the rooftop car park in his sports car. A few minutes later, Elichaoff 'jumped' to his death from the roof of the building. But did he jump or was he pushed? No one will ever know the truth. Police are convinced that the money laundering gang that had dominated London's financial underworld for at least the previous ten years played a direct role in Elichaoff's death.

Property deals, empty businesses – including sports franchises, movie production companies and even breweries – helped line the pockets of this particular money laundering gang as well as the huge fees they received from their clients for 'hiding' billions of pounds through those very same front activities.

A few months after Elichaoff's death in 2014, another man with links to the same mega-powerful London money laundering gang mysteriously fell to his death from a penthouse apartment in London's West End. The victim was grotesquely impaled on wrought iron railings one hundred feet beneath his balcony. Some even tried to claim the man threw himself off the balcony because he was consumed with guilt after talking to the police about his laundering gang associates.

Then a gang of old school professional criminals from London and the south east of England launched an audacious plan to try and take over London's lucrative laundering underworld from this established gang of professional money 'dealers'.

Tom explained: 'These guys were typical old school British criminals with backgrounds in armed robbery and drugs. They were convinced they had the right to earn a chunk of the laundering business because it was on their territory – London.'

As a result, a vicious turf war kicked off on the streets of the UK capital.

Tom went on: 'The old school guys were basically jealous because they'd heard these so called 'youngsters' were earning billions and they wanted a slice of it.'

In South London, in January 2015, Scotland Yard detectives were shadowing a member of one of the old school crime families trying to steal 'clients' from London's billionaire money laundering gang. The officers witnessed a hitman try to kill their surveillance target in broad daylight. He only survived because detectives called the emergency services immediately after they realised what was happening.

Just a few days later, in February 2015, six gangs of old school criminals met to agree to join forces to mount a full scale attack on the London billionaire laundering gang. The old timers were determined to wipe their young rivals off the face of the earth.

Tom explained: 'These old codger criminals didn't seem to appreciate that the billionaire gang of money launderers had the power and influence to destroy them if they wanted. It was stupid and ignorant of the old timers.'

Then in June 2015 in Brentwood, Essex, a contract killer shot dead one of these old school criminals in his own garden. The billionaire black money laundering gang behind the hit then deliberately spread rumours throughout the London underworld that the man was killed because he was about to inform on them.

* * *

But then came Brexit. The EU referendum in June 2016 and the result, with the British public voting to leave the European Union, changed everything. Not only was the political world in turmoil, but the financial world was flipped on its head as well, and the London billionaire laundering gang concluded it was only a matter of time before their lucrative operation collapsed. London was in financial freefall and other cities such as Bejing and Frankfurt were vying for the right to become the new dirty money capital of the world.

Tom went on: 'By this time these guys were financial wizards. They knew the writing was on the wall because of Brexit. But they had billions stashed away, which they could use to finance their exit strategy.'

So this London laundering gang closed down their entire operation virtually overnight. Leaders of the clan quietly departed the UK for 'safer' locations such as Monaco, Guernsey and the Cayman Islands, leaving London's black money underworld wide open once again. The old school criminals were soon touting their services as master money launderers.

Tom added: 'But the market died after the Brexit vote. That gang had literally fleeced London, made billions and then fucked off to their mansions in the sun. The old school guys might have thought they were back in charge but they'd completely missed the boat.'

Chapter 15

COUNTY LINES

'County Lines' is a term that should strike fear and trepidation into every law abiding citizen in Britain. It is a criminal phenomenon that threatens the very fabric of this nation's law and order system.

And it works like this: drug dealing gangs provide their customers with a branded mobile phone number to call whenever they want drugs. That number is controlled by a third party, who is not based in the marketplace but outside the county, hence the name, with the 'line' being the phone number used to obtain drugs. That criminal then contacts his dealers to arrange to drop off the drugs. Cloned phones are also used to further help avoid detection.

The key element to this criminal enterprise is mobility. The county lines system has meant UK criminals can set up drug hubs in communities hundreds of miles from their own headquarters.

A key feature of the county lines underworld is that group messages can also be sent out periodically to the customer base to advertise the availability of drugs and orders can even be placed back to this line in response. A relay system (involving another phone) is then used to pass orders onto dealers in the rural marketplace. But throughout this process, the branded phone line is controlled by senior gang members many miles away.

Police forces throughout the UK are now at war with the County Lines drug gangs. Many officers have even blamed the huge increase in knife murders across the UK in 2017/2018 on this ominous crime 'boom'.

Police say gangs are now using machetes, boiling water, knives, bats and hammers, resulting in broken and even amputated limbs, to set up County Lines drug supply hubs in cities and provincial towns and villages across the nation.

School children are even being lured into becoming drug smugglers by gangsters who promise them hundreds of pounds a week, a wide range of drugs and designer clothes, protection or perceived friendship or affection. Others get involved to stop someone carrying out a threat to harm their family.

The kind of violence and criminal activity normally associated with urban communities such as London, Manchester and Liverpool has spread to Middle England, thanks to these County Lines gangs.

The UK police say the majority of children recruited by county lines networks are between 14 and 16, but some areas young as 12. White British children of both sexes are often targeted, as gangs believe they're more likely to evade police detection. Social media, such as Facebook and Twitter, is also regularly used to make initial contact with children.

* * *

The city of Norwich, in Norfolk, is a classic County Lines target. London-based criminals have turned this once sleepy community into a crime-infested environment where guns are now used regularly by gangsters. Residents in the poorer areas of the city are often woken up at night by the sound of gunfire.

One former County Lines gang member called Ty explained: 'Norwich was a perfect target location as far as my gang was concerned. It's slightly cut off from other cities with lots of kids wanting to try drugs but unable to get their hands on much until we came along.'

Ty claimed he worked as a middle man between the young dealers operating in Norwich and his gang bosses back in East London.

Ty went on: 'The first thing any County Lines gang does is establish a secure storage hub where they can keep their drugs and all the cash proceedings. It was easy in Norwich because it has a lot of abandoned council flats in tower blocks that were perfect locations.'

This practice is called 'cuckooing'. Favoured locations in Norwich included apartments, holiday lets, budget hotels and even caravan parks where dealers can pick up drugs and drop off cash.

A recent shooting victim in Norwich turned out to be a 19–year–old from London. He'd been blasted in the back and buttocks in a classic county lines punishment shooting. And the people responsible for the attack were undoubtedly London gangster bosses based at the other end of the M11, which links Norwich to London.

Ty added: 'My gang bosses in London always used the threat of violence to keep everyone in check. If anyone stepped out of line they were severely punished in order to send a message out to others. And it worked most of the time.'

In Norwich – as in other cities – vulnerable teenagers, often in the care system, have been recruited by county lines drugs gangs as 'mules' to smuggle heroin and cocaine, by train or car, to surrounding towns and villages.

'The gang bosses back in London nurtured these sorts of people through social media. It was pretty easy because most of these types of kids need money desperately,' added Ty.

The drugs themselves were brought to Norwich from London, already saturated with drugs. The city was considered an untapped rural marketplace in which there were vast profits to be made.

Ty explained: 'Drugs were ordered in the same way you'd ring for a pizza. The order was taken by a guy in London, who would then call his 'salesman' in Norwich and a meeting would be arranged. If business was slow then cut-price deals ensured there were no shortage of customers. It's just like any business in a way. It all relies on supply and demand.'

And the county lines gangsters were able to thrive in some of Norwich's notoriously tough areas which had become over many years virtually no-go zones for the police.

As Ty went on: 'Norwich has these rundown areas where the County Lines gangs can operate safely. As I recall, it was one of the easiest places to set up shop.'

Chapelfield Gardens, in Norwich city centre, is just yards from the Theatre Royal and upmarket shops and restaurants. Its gardens dated from the 1880s and there was still a Victorian bandstand in the middle of the park. But today it is 'swamped' with drug dealers and their customers.

Ty explained: 'I rarely had to come into Norwich itself but one time there was a shortage of crack and I had to bring it in myself. I was astonished. Our dealers were operating literally a few yards from a busy city centre shopping area and the police were nowhere to be seen.'

Ty went on: 'I even recall there was a local kiosk in that same park serving tea and refreshments and it was where all the dealers congregated. Some of them were really young, no more than 14 or 15, and most of them were on pushbikes.'

Ty added: 'And you know what? They all talked like junior gangsters. Dressed in all the best designer gear and trainers. They even had manbags stuffed with cash, which they liked to show off by pulling out wads of money when they did a deal.'

Ty added: 'I told my bosses back in London I thought the Norwich operation was asking for trouble because the police were sure to eventually try and clear out the dealers.

'They laughed in my face because they weren't the ones taking any risks. It was the kids who were doing that. Even if the police did go in and bust the dealers (which they eventually did), it didn't matter to the gang bosses back in London because they were too far removed from it all to be nicked and they'd just set up another County Lines operation with some new kids.'

Ty explained: 'The young dealers were victims themselves in a sense. They came from care homes and had been ruthlessly exploited by the county lines gangs who'd come up from London and set things up.

The gang I worked for supplied crack cocaine and heroin in Norwich because they were the most addictive drugs. The idea was to hook in as many regular customers as possible. It's all about getting a foot in the door and then cashing in on the misery of others.'

One of the most disturbing aspects of the County Lines underworld is so-called 'plugging' which involves young criminals concealing drugs internally. This poses obvious health risks and there have been incidents of bags bursting, causing serious internal injuries and in some cases even death.

Ty explained: 'Plugging breaks all the usual criminal codes because these county lines gangsters have their own set of rules. Some of the young kids doing the dealing sometimes work for different gangs, depending on the availability of drugs at any given moment. I've even heard that sometimes gangs charged commission for allowing one of their dealers to work for another gang."

The other key ingredient in a County Lines gang is often the use of so-called 'clean skins'. These are people without a criminal record. Ty explained: 'Many of our recruits were missing persons, children in care or simply runaways because it's in their interests not to identify themselves accurately.'

County Lines gangs regularly target vulnerable individuals by attending recovery groups, dependency units and areas associated with social problems such as addiction and poverty in order to gain access to their homes, whether through grooming them, appearing to befriend them or issuing threats. Once they gain control over the victim, whether through drug dependency, debt or as part of their relationship, groups of criminals move in. The risk of domestic abuse, sexual exploitation and violence then hugely increases.

The final part of the County Lines operation involves using other groups of vulnerable youngsters to run bags of dirty money to specific locations where it can be laundered back into mainstream life.

Since the start of 2018, Norwich's drug problems have escalated even further. Ty explained: 'I got out of it all at the end of 2017 because I was very ill and so they dropped me from the gang. Thank goodness! Incredibly, they didn't try to recruit me and I've gone straight. Today, I look back on those far-off days as a bad dream. I shouldn't ever have got involved and I'm one of the few lucky ones to have got out in one piece.'

The police across Britain have been trying for more than two years to tackle the County Lines criminal phenomenon. But if Norwich is anything to go by, it is going to be an uphill struggle.

The police admit that trying to deal with the threat is like cutting a head off the mythical serpent Hydra.

As soon as one county line is closed down, another springs up.

Ty added: 'The County Lines gang bosses become like your parents in a sense. They own every aspect of your life but at the same time they provide you with the money that enables you to enjoy yourself. It's a fatal combination that can only lead to prison or death in the long run.'

Ty concluded: 'I suppose it's a bit like going to a school for villains. You learn how to survive on the streets, duck and dive and discover that those streets are the key to your own future. And of course it often leads to many of these youngsters moving into crime as a long-term career.'

Chapter 16

THE LADY COBRAS

On the face of it, Fancy is an ordinary mum who spends most of her year living with her family in north west London. In fact, she is part of Britain's booming drugs smuggling industry. According to the National Crime Agency, an estimated 25-30 tonnes of cocaine is imported into the UK every year. Fancy has played her own role in this, running a gang of female drugs mules known as 'the Lady Cobras', who smuggle 'product' between Jamaica and the UK.

On one occasion when she was younger, Fancy herself swallowed thirty pellets of cocaine and made it back to the UK to deliver the coke, despite one of the pullets bursting in her stomach. Now 43, Fancy has stepped back from the front line of drugs smuggling to run the Lady Cobras. Her story, and that of her gang, is both harrowing and fascinating because, from a criminal's perspective, the role of a mule epitomises the most dangerous aspect of the drug business.

Fancy admitted that her life has been hard, compounded by the fact that she has an ageing mother and two teenage children whom she's brought up as a single mother. But she insisted they have never suffered.

Fancy was adamant that she had always shunned the world of cocaine, until she met a man in London who became her lover. At the same time, he turned her into his mule 'slave.' She says: 'There's no other way to describe it. I loved this guy and I would do anything for him, even though I'm sure he didn't feel the same way about me. I was like putty in his hands.'

Only a few weeks after meeting her new lover, Fancy agreed to become a cocaine mule. She knew other friends who'd done it on their way back from seeing relatives in the Caribbean. The money was good and, as far as she was concerned, if it kept her man 'sweet' then it was worth the risk.

Fancy was eventually persuaded by her lover to help him recruit a gang of female mules with a promise that she could run the gang rather than work as a mule herself:

'There are people out there who will read this and think I'm the biggest cow in the world for putting people through this but it's not as if I haven't done it myself. My gang members are all women and they often need to go back to Jamaica to see their friends and relatives. It's a dream trip for them in a sense. And of course the money makes it worth it,' says Fancy.

As self-appointed leader of the Lady Cobras, Fancy has instigated a 'system' which is used for each run. She explained: 'Within days of confirming who we are using, I contact my gang partners in Jamaica so that our chosen mule can meet up with them once they've arrived on the island.'

'When my mule meets the supplier, the man gives her one cocaine pellet and asks her to swallow it. That's the test. If my mule can't swallow it the job's cancelled. When I was a mule myself I always got a bit nervous because that first pellet looked so big. But within minutes, it'd be fine. It's really no big deal once you know how to do it,' she added.

One of the gang's most recent mule runs involved a 30-year-old single mother called Charity. She arrived in Jamaica from London and then met up with her supplier.

Fancy explained: 'The trafficker gave Charity $500 to take care of some domestic expenses and to spruce up herself before she set out back for England the next day. Then she swallowed that first pellet there and then. This was to be followed by all the pellets the next morning before she went to the airport."

Pellets of drugs were always washed in bleach, soaked in a syrup-like solution and then kept in a refrigerator for several days to make them easier to swallow. Each packet of cocaine was supposed to have been tested to make sure that it was airtight by being floated in water. This indicated it would not unravel and leak in the stomach. "And if that happened the swallower would overdose and possibly die,' added Fancy in a matter of fact tone.

'But you have to trust the traffickers because they have the life of my girls in their hands,' explained Fancy. 'Once the pellets have been swallowed safely, the mules can drink anything – even hot stuff – without fear the pellets will burst. But if they're not wrapped properly you can't drink anything, you can't eat anything. You gotta be real careful.'

The next day, Fancy's gang member Charity swallowed another sixty-two pellets filled with cocaine in a cheap hotel room in downtown Kingston.

Fancy admitted mule flights back to London are always very stressful, as was the case for Charity. 'She told me later she couldn't stop worrying about what would happen if any of those pellets burst. It's quite natural but there's nothing we can do about it. This sort of stress comes with the territory.'

Charity later told Fancy she kept as still as she could throughout the flight from Kingston to London just in case the pellets did burst open into the stomach.

Fancy explained: 'Charity said she just kept thinking about the cash she would be paid and how it would help her kids and her mum. That's what drives on so many of the girls in the Lady Cobras. Often they've been left to bring up our kids alone on state benefits. Being a mule is the only way they can get one step ahead in terms of their finances.'

Fancy then explained how she arranged for Charity to be met at the airport in the UK by her lover. 'I did that deliberately because having her lover pick her up would make her feel more secure about everything,' said Fancy. 'It's also perfect because if she'd got stopped by customs she could talk to them all about her man waiting to meet her, and prove they were properly connected.'

In the case of Charity, once she'd safely left the airport, her lover took her to a house close to where they both lived in north west London. 'I know it feels a bit odd going into a complete stranger's house but that's how we do it,' explained Fancy. Once in the house, Charity's boyfriend gave her a laxative and milk to get her bowels moving. Then she visited the bathroom to start the process.

'He then gave her a bucket and gloves and disinfectant and she was told to wash and clean the pellets. It took about four hours to get all of them out,' explained Fancy. Minutes later, Charity was given an envelope with £3,000 in cash in it. Job done.

Fancy admitted many of her Lady Cobras end up blowing their 'fees' on drugs and partying. 'That's just

the way it is. Many of my girls simply live for today,'
said Fancy. 'I guess you could say the money fuels more
problems but it's not all spent this way. A lot of the girls
in the gang use it to look after their families as well.'

Fancy admitted that Charity's next mule 'run' did
not go so smoothly. 'Charity told me she needed more
money to pay some bills, so I fast tracked her onto
another job very quickly,' explained Fancy.

'I wanted to help her, we all need the money and
it's a pretty easy way to earn if you can handle the
stress. Of course we don't think about the people
whose lives are ruined by cocaine or the heavy guys
who kill people like us if we cross them.'

But on this occasion, it was almost Charity's life
that was ruined. 'A pellet split but luckily she got it
out in time,' explained Fancy. 'But Charity was so
freaked out that she decided to pull back for a bit. I
didn't blame her.'

Charity's decision to take a break from the mule
business sparked a lot of friction between Fancy and
Charity's lover, who usually greeted her at the airport.
'I told him I thought Charity should quit before something bad happened to her. He was angry. He thought
I had her under my control and now here I was advis-
ing her to stop working as a mule. Remember, he was
part of the 'supply chain', so if she stopped it would
cost him money.'

Over the following couple of months, gang boss Fancy and mule Charity went out of their way to avoid Charity's lover to try and put some distance between them and his cocaine gang. 'We deliberately avoided all the places where we thought he might show up. We didn't answer his calls. All my mates were telling us to hide for a bit. But it's not as easy as that. And then there was the money. Me and all the girls in the gang had got used to having a lot of cash.'

Late one evening, Charity's lover appeared at Fancy's front door demanding to come in. 'He was high on something and shouting and screaming at me. I knew what he was after and I tried to tell him to come back the next day. But he took no notice and just barged in. He said the drugs gang back in Jamaica were threatening to kill him for failing to get enough mules to work for him. He made it sound like they were really serious and his life was in danger. I fell for it. God knows why but I agreed to come out of retirement as a mule to do a run mainly to take the pressure off Charity, who was close to cracking up.'

Four days later Fancy herself arrived in Jamaica for what she promised her family would be the 'absolute last run'. Three days later she swallowed 100 pellets of cocaine and boarded the plane back to London.

As she sat down in her seat on the plane, Fancy thought she recognised among the passengers two women who worked as mules for other London gangs and suspected they might even be working for Charity's lover. After they touched down in London, Fancy made a point of not leaving the plane with them.

Fancy had just got through the main customs area at Heathrow and was turning the corner towards the exit when she was stopped by customs officials, who immediately asked her if she'd allow them to perform a body search.

Two female customs officers then took Fancy into a room and strip-searched her, but found nothing. They went through her luggage carefully but still came up with nothing. Then one customs officer told Fancy they felt she had something inside her and invited her to do a urine test. She agreed. 'What else could I do?' Fancy later explained.

Fancy was then taken into another room and given a blue book, which contained the rights and rules of British customs and immigration laws. Fancy says she pushed the book away but they insisted she signed it, which she eventually did. Then they gave her ten cups of water followed by three cups of hot tea.

Fancy was escorted upstairs to a toilet, which was transparent and had a large transparent Perspex hose linking it to a sink. 'I was very scared but I tried hard not to show it. I kept thinking about my kids and how they'd suffer if I ended up in prison. And of course

I greatly regretted running the mule gang in London in the first place. I had been such a fool. I saw my whole life flashing in front of me and I felt so low and ashamed of everything.'

Fancy asked the customs officers if she could have something to eat but before she got an answer, one officer came back with the result of the urine test. 'By this time, I was I exhausted and terrified. This was the moment I'd always dreaded and if I hadn't been such a fool and thought I could get away with it one last time, I wouldn't have found myself sitting there waiting for them to put the handcuffs on.'

The officer looked down at Fancy as she walked around and around the table Fancy was sitting at. 'The suspense was killing me so I looked up at her and said, "Well?" She looked really pissed off and just mumbled "You're free to leave."

'I couldn't believe my ears. I looked at her, waiting for her to say she was kidding but she didn't say another word. I'd passed! I have no idea to this day how I got away with it but I did.'

Fancy claims she 'learned a lot of lessons' that day. 'I finally saw the consequences of my actions and those of the women in my gang. So many people suffered because of my stupidity and greed. It was an awakening in many ways. I went to the trafficker's house, emptied the contents of my stomach and slapped him harder than I have ever hit anyone in my life. He was so shocked he didn't retaliate. I walked out of there and told him never to contact me or my girls ever again. I'd finally come to my senses and realised that running a mule gang was the ultimate form of exploitation. How could I have done such a terrible thing?'

Luckily for Fancy, the trafficker backed off and didn't press her or her gang members to do any further 'work' for him again. She explained: 'I like to think he recognised that my gang and all the women in it did not deserve to be pulled into such a dark place. But, hey, who knows?'

Fancy knows how lucky she and her mule gang members were not to be arrested, or killed by the deadly 'shipment' of cocaine pellets they carried in their stomachs. She also speculated that the traffickers were still running teams of mules from Jamaica to London. 'And I'm sure one or two of them will die and others will end up in jail. We are the secret victims of all this.'

Today, Fancy firmly believes it is now her 'duty' to make sure that people understand the risks and dangers of being a mule. 'You often don't get the money they promise in the first place,' she says. 'They rip you off and they don't care if you live or die. It's really not worth it. I promise you.'

Despite her experiences, Fancy has never once considered going to the police to help them gather enough evidence to expose the drug trafficking gangs, who first persuaded her to work as a mule and then encouraged her to set up the Lady Cobras in London.

'I couldn't shop the drugs gang to the police because that would have been crossing a line where I come from. Maybe that's why that trafficker didn't come after me or Charity when we finally refused to work for him ever again. He knew we would never inform on him. It's just not the way things are done where we come from.

'In any case, even if the police had arrested him and his gang, another gang would have replaced them just like another gang of mules have replaced my operation. People want this stuff like they want petrol for their cars and food for their tables. As long as the demand continues there will always be bad men prepared to force people like myself and my friends to smuggle cocaine in our stomachs.'

Meanwhile, Fancy has got herself a full-time job as an assistant in a children's nursery near her home. 'I love kids and I want to help them. This is the first time in my life I have a job that helps others. It's a much better feeling than swallowing pellets of cocaine and sitting on a plane for ten hours or making others do that. I may not earn much money but I go home every night feeling a lot better about myself.'

Chapter 17

OLD SCHOOL

In the Kent countryside, a few old school British mobsters continue to run their gangs from isolated farmhouses and mansions that provide easy access to the cross-Channel ports of Dover and Folkestone.

Stan is one of this shady underworld's most famil-iar faces and he told me that today's up-and-coming young cocaine gangs are in danger of turning parts of the UK into deadly no-go areas.

'It's all got completely fuckin' out of hand in recent years,' explained Stan, smoking a king-size cigar and supping a vodka and tonic. 'The gangs coming through the ranks now are full of complete and utter psychos. It's bedlam out there and a lot of innocent people are being knocked off for no good reason. This country is turning into the Wild fuckin' West.'

Stan, now in his late sixties, believes his gang of 'old chaps' only get any respect from the younger cocaine gangsters in the UK because of their notorious pasts. 'We've got form going way back,' explained Stan. By 'form', he means that he has been in prison for killing a criminal rival and was also busted for running one of the UK's biggest cocaine gangs in the late 1990s.

Stan insists that today he and his gang are still free to move around the south coast of England without fear of retribution from rival gangsters. 'In fact some of the so-called new boys come to me for advice,' said Stan between puffs on his fat cigar. 'But a lot of my old mates are shit scared to be seen out and about in case they cop a bullet from this lot.'

He went on: 'I'd been in the coke game for thirty years when some of these foreign gangs began turning up here a few years back. I told my mates in the business to watch out because where they come from, life is cheap and they've had it hard. That makes them much colder and more inclined to shoot first and ask questions later, if you know what I mean.'

Stan believes he and his gang occupies a relatively safe 'middle ground' between the old and new drugs gangs operating in the South East of England.

'There's a couple of younger gangs working on my manor, so I went to see them and told them straight that I didn't expect any of them to interfere with my operations and in exchange I'd keep out of their business. All the other old boys I know said I was barking mad to front them up. But I reckon it's paid off handsomely. I really do. I sat down with the youngsters and we came to an agreement. That's all I ever wanted. What's the point in havin' a ruck? It don't help no one does it?'

When I met Stan at his favourite pub, overlooking a marina on the outskirts of a small Kent coastal town, he claimed he'd just come from a meeting with a man who represented a foreign billionaire residing in London. 'He's on the make like all the rest of them,' explained Stan, wearing his favourite country gent 'uniform' of tweed jacket, checked trousers and brogues.

Stan had met the billionaire's 'rep' at a safehouse, just up the road from the marina. 'This bloke had five body-guards. Can you believe it? He wanted to invest some of his boss's cash in the coke game and expected me to tell him about what sort of return he could get for his money. I get these types of characters coming to me all the time these days. I tend to avoid them, unless they're real professionals because they don't really understand the risks. They just think it's a just a simple way to wash dirty money and make an easy buck. But it's not.'

The bar we were talking in was decked out in garish, swirly wallpaper and looked as if it hadn't had a lick of paint since the days when Stan first began 'investing' drugs money, buying property in the London Docklands development during the reign of Margaret Thatcher in the mid-eighties.

As we were talking, a burned out looking blonde woman in her late forties in tight jeans glanced across at Stan and smiled. He winked back and then contin-ued with his overview of the cocaine gang wars raging in south east England. 'It's changing all the time. A lot of the older Brits have left England and retired to Thailand and Costa Rica and places like that because it's too fuckin' crowded here these days. Spain's too near and it's not cheap any more. You're better off further away from Blighty.'

In that case, why was Stan still in the UK?

'Me and my gang have avoided these shoot-ups and shit like that. In any case, I've been bedded down here for so long I wouldn't know how to survive anywhere else.' And survival is the key word here. For Stan's primary skill still seems to be ducking and diving his way out of trouble.

He recalled: 'About a year ago this gang of Albanian coke traffickers turned up in a village near my place and started giving it large in all directions. They rented a farmhouse, a couple of Mercedes and shipped in hookers most nights and gave the impression they were made men. Then a gang of Bulgarians I know heard about them.

'Well, if there's one thing the Bulgarians don't like, it's the Albanians. They made it their business to run them out of town. These particular Bulgarians employed a team of fruitcake Moldovan ex-paratroopers as bodyguards and they charged up the driveway to the Albanians' farmhouse one night, sprayed it with bullets and then left a couple of firebombs behind for good measure. The Albanians got the message and were never seen again.'

Stan made light of it all, but there was a serious point to what he was saying. 'I take the attitude that hopefully they'll all wipe each other out. Then once the dust has settled maybe I'll stroll back in and start expanding my business again.'

Stan says his main priority is to make sure his face doesn't end up looking like he's been in a car crash. 'I've always been a bit of a diplomat. I pride myself on not clashing with other villains. It just ain't worth it.'

A few days later, I found myself in another of Stan's favourite watering holes, this time in the suburbs of south London. At least half a dozen of the customers reeked of criminality. Most of them were watching Premiership football on Sky Sports in the corner of the bar. Then, as evening drew in, they began rushing to the toilet to take cocaine and eventually they were all extremely hyped up.

'They're all at it,' said Stan, as we sat in a corner of the bar. 'That's the biggest problem. No one can go out for a quiet pint no more. It's gotta be a bottle of voddie and a packet of Charlie. No wonder there is such demand for the fuckin' stuff. Everyone's on it these days.'

As darkness fell and the chemicals kicked in, some of the villains sitting nearby flexed their muscles a bit and looked around to see who was watching them. The atmosphere in that pub in the suburbs was more akin to a scene from *Goodfellas*, with one particularly coked-up little character, who look a bit like Robert de Niro, marching in and out of the gents almost every two minutes to replenish his nostrils.

'In the old days they'd have chopped it all out on the table, but the landlord has told them to keep it low key cos quite a few cozzers have been using this place recently,' explained Stan.

We were in this particular pub to meet Vlad, a 'foreigner mate' of Stan's, whom he claimed was 'a good example of a decent foreigner running a so-called 'clean' gang, not like the rest of them.'

Vlad described himself as a 'Latvian businessman'. He'd lived in Kent for three years. He clearly respected Stan and the two seemed close. 'The trouble with you Brits is that you drink too much and you take too much cocaine,' said Vlad. Stan sitting next to him laughed loudly. 'I told you didn't I?'

Vlad continued: 'Where I come from we can hold our drink and we don't take drugs because then we are not in control.'

I soon discovered why Vlad was the only non-British man in the pub that night. It turned out that he employed half the British old school gangsters in there to help him run his 'businesses'.

Vlad explained: 'I like the Brits. I like your way of life. The loyalty. The humour. I don't trust my countrymen, especially when they're here in the UK. They would kill you as soon as look at you if you had something they wanted.'

Vlad then went on to provide a new perspective on the cocaine gangs of the south east's underworld. 'There are many more opportunities here than in our home countries, so we come here. It's as simple as that.'

He went on: 'You Brits think you live in such a civilised place with so little crime compared with other countries. Well let me tell you here and now, it's easier to run a cocaine gang here than in my country. Less cops to blackmail you for starters!'

'In any case, people have more money here and that means more opportunities for guys like me. But I'm not a typical foreign criminal. I respect this country and I don't want to turn it into a battlefield. I'm afraid others are not as considerate as me.

'Sure I sometimes have to make an example of my enemies. I don't like doing it but in the long term it helps stop a lot of what I will call "unfortunate incidents".'

Vlad refused to elaborate on exactly what 'action' he'd taken in the past, but suffice to say it must have resulted in someone being physically harmed.

Surely, I asked, the police are a problem? 'As I said, the police cannot be bought so easily here but,' he shrugged, 'there are always some who will accept money.' Vlad claimed that one Kent detective offered to 'work' for him exclusively while continuing to serve in the police. 'I wasn't surprised,' said Vlad. 'He'd just got divorced and needed to earn more money in order to pay off his ex-wife. We all have these problems. But I was suspicious of this guy, so I turned down his offer. A few months later he helped bust another foreign gang. He'd been undercover. I had been right all along.'

Vlad believes the police can do little to prevent the production lines of new gangs emerging in the UK. 'The cops don't have the manpower or the resources to investigate every gang,' explained Vlad. 'It's almost as if they're happy for us to continue bringing money into the economy because it means a better life for a lot of people in this area. They need us here. It's been like this for so long the whole place would collapse if criminals were not operating here.'

Both Stan and Vlad claim many of the gangs based in and around England's Home Counties are also involved in prostitution, robbery and fraud. 'It's not just drugs,' said Vlad. There are other 'activities'. I personally don't like this. I want our streets to be clean and safe for our children and grandchildren to play on. Also, I want our banks to be good at not losing our money, eh?' Vlad laughs and slaps his friend Stan on the thigh.

I wondered whether Stan was now working for Vlad. But even if he was, I knew he would never have admitted to it.

Conclusion

It seems that the UK's criminal underworld has been fundamentally changed by a lethal combination of cocaine and foreign criminals, and, terrifyingly, there is absolutely no sign of this slowing down.

One retired London gangster told me ten years ago that 'Being British doesn't mean anything anymore'. This sentiment couldn't be any more relevant today, and the criminal landscape of this country would be entirely foreign to the gangsters of old, who operated from within their manor, inspiring fear but also a sense of respect from their community

As you've seen, the prevalence of gangs operating in our country is only increasing, and their deadly reach is now able to extend to areas of the country that rarely found themselves touched by crime.

Our police forces trying to crack these gangs have a harder task on their hands than ever before, with the crime industry becoming ever more secretive, using encrypted messaging, the Dark Web, or just a simple phone number to connect dealers to a whole new market to exploit.

And to add to all of this, is Brexit. Not only is it the biggest political issue of our time, but one that has huge consequences for the nation's gangs. Already, there are gang wars intensifying to control land around our ports and borders as various foreign and British gangs vie to take charge of their patch.

As the public mood begins to shift and ordinary, law-abiding people see the realities of crime spilling into their day-to-day lives, with daily news alerts of another teenager's life cut short or headlines telling us that knife crime is rising at a faster rate outside London than inside it, there's an increasing feeling that something has to change.

However, as we've seen, Britain's gangs are inventive, wily and excellent at operating in secret as they find a new way to make money. In these turbulent times, who can say where it will all end?